FRANTZ FANON

MODERN MASTERS

EDITED BY frank kermode

frantz fanon

david caute

NEW YORK | THE VIKING PRESS

ACKNOWLEDGMENT

Grove Press, Inc.: From *The Wretched of The Earth* by Frantz Fanon. Translated from the French by Constance Farrington. Copyright © 1963 by Présence Africaine. Published by Grove Press, Inc.

I should like to thank Mr. Chris Allen,
Mr. Donal Cruise O'Brien, and Mr. Martin Staniland,
who were kind enough to read the text
and who made many helpful suggestions.

CONTENTS

BIOGRAPHICAL NOTE

1925	Born in the French Antilles. Subsequently attended schools in Martinique and France.
1944	Volunteered for the Army and served in Europe.
1945–1950	Studied medicine and psychiatry at Lyons. Editor of *Tom-Tom*, mimeographed newspaper for black students.
1951	Medical dissertation.
1952	Publication of *Peau noire, masques blancs*, Paris.
1953	Married. Appointed Head of the Psychiatric Department, Blida-Joinville Hospital, Algeria.
1954	Algerian Revolution begins.
1954–1956	Aided Algerian rebels.
1956	Resigned from Blida-Joinville Hospital. Attended First Congress of Black Writers and Artists, Paris. Took up editorial post on the FLN newspaper, *El Moudjahid*, Tunis.
1957–1958	Attended inter-African congress at Bamako and Cotonou.

1959   Seriously injured by a mine on the Algerian-Moroccan frontier.

Publication of *L'an V de la révolution algérienne*, Paris.

1960   Appointed Ambassador of the Algerian Provisional Government to Ghana.

Journey to Mali to explore southern supply routes to Algeria. Evaded French kidnaping attempt.

Contracted leukemia. Medical treatment in the USSR.

1961   Publication of *Les damnés de la terre*, Paris.

(December) Died in hospital in Washington, D.C.

Buried in Algeria.

1962   Algerian independence.

1964   Publication of *Pour la révolution africaine*, Paris.

FRANTZ FANON

Black Skin, White Masks

i

This is how Frantz Fanon begins. "I am talking of millions of men who have been skillfully injected with fear, inferiority complexes, trepidation, servility, despair, abasement."

The words are borrowed from Aimé Césaire, poet and politician: Césaire, like Fanon, a "citizen" of France; Césaire, like Fanon, a native of Martinique; Césaire, like Fanon, black.

"I am *talking of* millions of men. . . ." By the end of his short life Fanon was *speaking for* millions of men. He spoke for the black Antilles, for Algeria, and for black Africa with the same inexorable logic and the same transparent love of justice with which Guevara spoke for the peasants and peons of Latin America, but not without paradox and tragedy—paradox because the doctrines of Fanon and Guevara are today better known to Europeans and

Americans than to *les damnés de la terre* whose revolutionary cause they championed; tragedy because poverty, exploitation, and oppression remain the basic facts of life for the majority of the world's inhabitants. No doubt it can be argued that Fanon and Guevara have been inflated into the exaggerated dimensions of charismatic idols. In an overturned, humane world, a global society harmonized by abiding principles of equity and mutual respect among men, the mystique of the prophet would no longer be relevant. Karl Marx was "created" by capitalism; Garibaldi by Sicilian poverty; Lenin by the Russian autocracy; Gandhi by British imperialism. Fanon was created by the white man.

Yet this is not quite true. Although Fanon's predicament, his situation, was environmentally defined, the same cannot be said for his thought, his life, the man he made of himself. There is always a choice. Fanon had every opportunity to allow himself to become assimilated into the middle-class black elite which the French colonial system carefully nurtured. But some distinctive personal quality, some force of temperament, pulled him back from the consequences of his own skills and achievements. He became a rebel, then a revolutionary.

The Guevara of black Africa? The parallel would not be exact. Guevara's identity and stature derive essentially from the fusion of the activist and theoretician, the guerrilla leader and the writer. Fanon, it is true, became an active militant in the course of the Algerian war of liberation and in the cause of African freedom, but in this capacity his achievements were not outstanding. It is on the basis of his writings—most of them made widely available only since his death in 1961—that his growing influence and appeal rest.

Black Africa finds its nearest counterpart to Guevara in Amílcar Cabral, the mulatto agronomist and revolutionary theoretician who has led the successful guerrilla campaigns in Portuguese Guinea and the Cape Verde Islands. Certainly a Senghor, a Sékou Touré, a Nkrumah, have combined practical political abilities with a flair for theory, but these leaders, however salient their role in national independence movements, found their natural arena in the urban market place and not in the jungles and remote mountain retreats. Time and the practice of power have tarnished their original idealism—this is also the case with Césaire. Guevara was apparently not interested in high office. Would Fanon have been? We cannot know. He had become by the end of his life an intransigent revolutionary idealist; such men are restless.

Throughout his life, Fanon was plagued and embittered by his encounters with racism. As a young man he had believed that he could break through the color barrier on the strength of his education and personal capacities. He volunteered for the French Army during the war and found himself in Europe from 1944. Later he studied medicine and psychiatry at Lyons, and it was here that he began to realize that for the French a Negro, regardless of his level of education and culture, was always primarily a Negro—and therefore inferior. "When people like me, they tell me it is in spite of my color. When they dislike me, they point out that it is not because of my color. Either way, I am locked into the infernal cycle."[1] A university examiner addressed him with insulting familiarity as *"tu"*: *"Et toi, d'où es-tu? . . . Ah! La Martinique: beau pays . . ."* (At about the same time, thousands of miles away, the young

[1] Frantz Fanon, *Black Skin, White Masks* (New York, 1967), p. 116.

Patrice Lumumba, who was born in the same year as Fanon—1925—and who died in the same year—1961 —happened by mistake to knock into a white woman in the streets of Léopoldville. She turned on him, furious: *"Tu ne peux pas faire attention, sale macaque?"*) The examination system at Lyons was for the candidate to plunge his hand into a basket and to pull out a question at random, but the examiner asked Fanon patronizingly, "What do you want me to question you about?" Fanon plunged his hand into the basket.

Despite these humiliations, he gained high qualifications, married a Frenchwoman, and was appointed Head of the Psychiatric Department of the Blida-Joinville Hospital in Algeria. This was in 1953. But his skin remained black. In later years, in Italy, it was always his wife who booked the hotel rooms. Fanon's bitter bewilderment might have been lessened had this kind of prejudice been confined to white Europe alone, but even within the "Third World," supposedly united by its struggle against colonialism, he continued to encounter the virus. Simone de Beauvoir recalls, "In Tunis, the eyes that turned to watch him in the street never let him forget the color of his skin." The dialectic of racism and counter-racism, once set in motion, is apparently irreversible; in Guinea, Fanon's African friends could not bring themselves to hold important conversations with him in the presence of his white wife.

In a French (or British, or Dutch, or Portuguese) colony ruled by white men, a white skin is associated with power, status, wealth, superiority. This association is not symbolic; it is rooted in the social structure. In Fanon's native Martinique the French language, French education, French culture, and French religion all became primary targets of attainment for the Negroes. The Negroes are descended from black slaves transported from Africa to work on the sugar and coffee plantations; the Negroes wish to forget this. The official French policy of assimilation is colorblind; the Negroes wish to believe this.

In *Black Skin, White Masks*, Fanon describes the many techniques, some of them only semiconscious, by which the black native is persuaded to feel and live his inbred racial guilt. In the Antilles as in France, school-children were reared on stories in which the black man symbolized the forces of evil. It was all very well to go to the movies in Fort-de-France and to laugh at the wild antics of Bushmen and Zulus, to support Tarzan against the malevolent blacks, but to sit in a French cinema in the face of the same rubbish was a petrifying experience. In the context of a white audience, the Negro, whether he liked it or not, found himself identified with the Bushmen and Zulus. He was condemned.

So the Negroes of the Antilles aspired to be white, to be French. The middle classes never spoke Creole, except to their servants. They spoke French. Far from joyfully exploring their African ancestry, the West Indian bourgeoisie resolutely despised Negroes who arrived from Dahomey or Senegal. Whereas the Africans formed separate army regiments, the West Indians were proud to serve in European units. The middle-class West Indian, arriving in France, did all in his power to suppress his identity as a Negro. "Negroes," he insisted, were Africans, whereas he himself was a cultivated, assimilated European who happened to be colored. But the color of his skin was so irrelevant that it vanished; he wore a white mask. For their part, the whites stubbornly clung to their archetypal image of the pidgin-speaking nigger, the grinning golliwogg, even when confronted with a Fanon who spoke their language perfectly. They sealed the Negro into his blackness.

This psychosocial structure was reflected, as Fanon explains, in painful sexual neuroses. The black male West Indian arriving at Le Havre hurried from his boat to a brothel where he could taste, for the first time, the flesh of the white female. "When my restless hands caress those white breasts, they grasp white civilization and dignity and make them mine."[2] In his autobiography, Malcolm X dismisses as a lie and white myth the notion that the Negro's prime desire is to possess a white woman. But Malcolm's disciple Eldridge Cleaver describes his former obsessional drive toward white womanhood and the rejection by the majority of his fellow black prison convicts of women of their own race. The "restless hands" to which Fanon alludes were willingly received for a payment, but Cleaver's shame and guilt drove him finally to deliberate, premeditated rape, viewed as "an insurrectionary act." Cleaver, like Fanon before him, had read Richard Wright's novel *Native Son*. Now he did what the novel's simple hero, Bigger Thomas, had not done but what the white world insisted he had done—play out the role of black, primeval beast by wanton rape.

And there lies a significant development. The black French *évolué* (relatively educated, Europeanized, and privileged), hungry for dignity, respect, equality and integration, would have regarded such an act as inconceivable. A decade later, the young black intellectual in America, totally despairing of these ideals, takes defiant refuge in the image which the white man has imposed on him. Fanon recalls that in his profes-

[2] *Ibid.*, p. 63.

sional capacity as a doctor he questioned, over a three-
or four-year period, some five hundred whites of different European nationalities. Over sixty per cent re-
acted to the word "Negro" by associating it with boxer,
biology, penis, strong, athletic, savage, animal, devil,
sin. And Fanon points out that if he, as interrogator,
had been white, the percentage would undoubtedly have
been higher. Just as money or cunning had come to
symbolize the subversive power of the Jews, so sexual
potency symbolized that of the Negroes. But Fanon, the
French man of science, goes on to insist that Negro
sexual prowess, whether measured anatomically or in
terms of performance, is a myth. The black American,
perpetually thwarted from fulfilling his masculinity in
terms of economic or social power, finally embraces
the substitute, the stereotype of himself as athletically
and sexually superior to the white man.[3] Meanwhile the
French or British Negro continues his search for integration, or, alternatively, for the political authority
and self-respect which decolonization in Africa offers
him.

But the sexual tension is not confined to the black
male. The black girl also nurses her dreamlike quest
for what Cleaver calls her "psychic bridegroom."
Fanon devotes painful pages to an exploration of the
West Indian girl's search for a white husband or, more
realistically, for a mate blessed with the lightest possible skin. The black girl of Martinique has only one
concern—to turn white; the mulatto girl must at all
costs avoid slipping back into blackness. And in America too black girls have for generations been brought
up to regard themselves as ugly and deficient—hence
the protracted agonies of hair-straightening with oil

[3] *See* W. H. Grier and P. M. Cobbs, *Black Rage* (New York,
1968).

and hot combs, the hours spent with bleaching creams. But that is also changing. In Agnès Varda's short film, *Black Panther*, Kathleen Cleaver appears with a great dome of tight, wiry hair crowning her head. "It's beautiful," she says.

Did the Negroes of Martinique at some stage manage to transcend their humiliating efforts at what Fanon called "lactification"? A traumatic blow to the unreal assumptions of a group or individual can result in a rapid disintegration of the white mask. Only a few years before he became the radical Prime Minister of the Congo, Patrice Lumumba had submitted himself to the degrading *immatriculation*, by which every aspect of the life of *évolué* was investigated in order to determine whether he had achieved European levels of civilization. Then Lumumba was imprisoned; when he regained his freedom, his heart was black—black with rage, but also black. As regards the Antilles, Fanon's testimony presents an ambiguity if not a straight contradiction. The servile, assimilationist, "white masks" attitude he depicts in his first book, published in 1952, is clearly intended to portray the situation as it then stood. (He uses the present tense throughout.) But in an article published in 1955,[4] he takes up a historical perspective and argues that the Second World War in fact provided a turning point in French West Indian collective psychology.

Before 1939, he says, there were no more than two thousand Europeans permanently resident in Martinique. They had specific jobs and they had a specific place in society. Then, with the war and the fall of France, there suddenly arrived ten thousand European refugees, mainly sailors, in Fort-de-France. These men

[4] Fanon, "Antillais et Africains," *Pour la révolution africaine* (Paris, 1964), p. 27.

lived in exile for four years, inactive, closed in on themselves, full of despair; they became authentically racist. The blacks had no choice but to defend themselves. When previously Aimé Césaire had declared, "How good and beautiful it is to be black," he had caused a scandal, a shock to the collective unconscious; blacks and whites alike took him to be mad. But now his teaching gained converts. A new respect for blackness—for black skin, black art, black primitivism—developed, and with it a new political radicalism. Two out of the three parliamentary deputies sent by Martinique to Paris after the Liberation were Communists; one of them was Césaire. Now, continues Fanon, West Indians hurried to Senegal full of hope, eager to grasp the black breasts of mother Africa. Arriving in Dakar, they were distressed to find the roles reversed, to find themselves rejected as not black enough. But this black rejection, like the white European one that preceded it, only intensified their efforts: this time they wore Negro masks.

Now historically both accounts cannot be equally true. The discrepancy, I would suggest, can best be explained in terms of two Fanonian attributes: his rationalist-abstract methodology, and the normative perspective of a strongly programatic writer.

Fanon was French, and he wrote within a certain French philosophical tradition. Whereas the postwar writers from the British West Indies have gravitated naturally toward the novel as a means of conveying the particularities of racial confrontation in all their subtlety, variance, and ambiguity, Fanon's literary culture was abstract, didactic, and often rhetorically assertive. There is a common slang phrase in currency today—"Tell it like it is." Fanon, working in the existentialist-phenomenological perspective of Sartre, Merleau-Ponty, and, more obliquely, Camus, always aims for the heart of the matter. He cuts through the confusing myriad of surface details. *This*, he insists, is like it really *is*. With an English-language West Indian novelist such as, for example, V. S. Naipul, the hero we first encounter is a person called Mr. Biswas; only gradually, hesitantly, ambiguously, do we learn about Mr. Biswas' color, job, status, and attitudes. But Fanon deals in essentialist categories—"the black," "the white," "the colonizer," "the colonized," "the native," "the racist," "the peasant," "the bourgeois." Fanon's thought moves with impatience from the individual man into Hegelian categories—"subject and object," "self and other"—categories which are often put to gloriously illuminating dialectical work but which sometimes shine too brightly with a spurious clarity.

Therefore he sometimes exaggerates. Just as, in *Black Skin, White Masks*, he exaggerated the ubiquity of the white-mask psychology among West Indians, so in 1955 he exaggerated the prevalence of the reverse black-mask psychology. And this is because Fanon was, and declared himself to be, a didactic writer, concerned to project a particular subjectivity and to change or modify the world in the process. Sartre had described committed literature as a form of action, action by disclosure, and Fanon invariably uses the written word as a tool. In his first book, he was attempting to break the seal of the white man's whiteness and of the black man's blackness. By 1955, having witnessed the outbreak of the Algerian revolution and become increasingly aware of the rising independence movements in the black colonies, his project had become that of a political militant. Consequently he was concerned to explore the historical roots of an emerging black political ideology. Fanon's method is to fuse the descriptive and the normative, to put the "like it is" at the service of the "like it ought to be."

In 1952 he was still dedicated to integration on the basis of equality. The black man discards his dreams of integration when he learns two things: first, that by integration the white man means "be like me"; second, that the white man is convinced that the black man can never be like him, can never be as good as he is. When the black man finally absorbs the second point he begins to question the first. Then he decides, like James Baldwin, that "there is no reason for you to try to become like white people and there is no basis whatever for their impertinent assumption that *they* must accept *you*."[5] But in his first book Fanon had not yet reached this terminus, which is also a point of departure. He regarded the colonized Negro's tendency toward insularity and ego-withdrawal (according to the formula of Anna Freud) as unworkable. The Negro required and justified white acceptance. "However painful it may be for me to accept this conclusion, I am obliged to state it: For the black man there is only one destiny. And it is white." And he added, "It was not the black world that laid down my course of conduct. My black skin is not the wrapping of specific values."[6]

What laid down his course of conduct was the phenomenon of colonialism. Martinique had been a French possession since 1625. Even in his first book Fanon's approach to colonialism is one of extreme hostility: it was an act of economic pillage, brute force, political tyranny, and psychological emasculation. Césaire had described it as *"chosification"* (turning men into things). Fanon agreed: to enslave men it was necessary to divest them of their humanity by systematic mystifica-

[5] J. Baldwin, *The Fire Next Time* (New York, 1963), p. 16.
[6] Fanon, *Black Skin, White Masks*, pp. 12 and 227.

tion. Of course, not all manifestations of racism were specifically colonial in the orthodox sense. Anti-Semitism was a case in point. But, says Fanon, the effect is analogous. Had not Hitler and the Nazis handed out to Europe the same imperialist subjugation, complete with racist psychoses, that the virtuous and democratic European nations had all along been inflicting on their colonial peoples? This argument, a sound one, is evidently taken up from Césaire's thrust that Hitler's crime had been to humiliate the white man in the same way that the white man had humiliated the black. Césaire quotes the greatly respected Renan: "The regeneration of inferior or degenerate races by the superior races is the providential order of humanity." If there was a distinction between regeneration and subjugation, the "native" would be the last to notice it. Fanon was adamant on the matter: a society is either racist or it is not. "Colonial racism is no different from any other racism." For a Jew, the differences between the anti-Semitism of a Charles Maurras and that of a Goebbels were "imperceptible."

One wonders about this. The difference might in practice amount to life or death. Fanon was much impressed by the phenomenological arguments used by Sartre in *Anti-Semite and Jew*. The Jew, said Sartre, let himself be poisoned by the hostile stereotype that others had of him, and, in the strenuous attempt to avoid acting in accordance with this stereotype, robbed himself of his own authenticity. Thus his conduct was "overdetermined" (*surdéterminé*) from the inside. Fanon noted that whereas the Jew can often pass unnoticed in the company of white Gentiles, the black is damned by his skin; his victimization is both predetermined and "overdetermined" from the outside. Furthermore, while the Jew is "the Other" to the prejudiced Gentile, the black is not only "the Other" to the white man; he is also slave to the master. This being the case, Fanon's insistence that colonial racism is not different from any other form of racism appears to be contradicted.

Fanon himself points out that the prevailing form of racism is determined by the general cultural system of which it is part and by the historical circumstances which engender the specific culture. In his address to the First Congress of Black Writers and Artists, held in Paris in September 1956, he observed that certain crude forms of racism were on the way out, particularly those based on physical criteria such as the shape of the head, the dimensions of the vertebrae, cell formations, and so forth. He offered by way of example the work of the French scholar Porot, who in 1935 described the North African as typically having only poorly developed cortical activities and being primarily regulated by the diencephalon. (Compared to other vertebrates, human beings are highly corticalized; the diencephalon is a primitive part of the brain.) Fanon correlated this biological racism with a specific period of colonial exploitation when the "native" was harnessed like a human mule for his brute muscle-power. However, he noted that an official of the World Health Organization had concluded as late as 1954 that "the African makes very little use of his frontal lobes" and that the typical African was a "lobotomized European." This kind of racism—if we are concerned with cause and effect— was also prevalent in nineteenth-century Germany as a means of differentiating "Aryans" from Jews, although it could hardly be argued that the Jew's typical role in German society was that of muscular menial.

According to Fanon, the development of more sophisticated economic techniques and the consequent creation of skilled and semiskilled cadres among the colonized peoples result in a more subtle form of racial disparagement. Aboriginal culture is paid tribute by white ethnologists—who depict it in exotic colors, often with sentimental affection—as the authentic form of expression of an inherently static and simple people. Thus apathy and inertia are encouraged, and the dynamics of social change blocked.

Fanon here chose as his principal target the work of a French anthropologist, O. Mannoni.[7] Mannoni, who had made a protracted study of black society in Madagascar, concluded that the natural historical psychology of the Malagasy people was one of "dependence." The coming of the white colonizer had been anticipated in local legends, and the colonial relationship that ensued could be attributed to the encounter between two distinct racial personalities. The whites instinctively grasped for mastery and power as the only escape from a sense of "inferiority" and "unsatisfaction" (a form of overcompensation, following Adler's formula), while the Malagasy society naturally transferred its dependency complex from traditional sources of authority to the new ones. Mannoni speculated that a "dependence complex" might be the psychological key to all backward peoples whose civilizations had stagnated. "To my mind there is no doubting that colonization has always required the existence of the need for dependence. Not all peoples can be colonized: only those who experience this need."[8] As for the Malagasy revolt of 1947, bloodily suppressed by the French, Mannoni explained that the revolt had followed the granting of concessions which left the blacks half free, half un-

---

[7] O. Mannoni, *Prospero and Caliban: The Psychology of Colonization.* Translated by P. Powesland (New York, 1956).
[8] *Ibid.*, p. 85.

free, and which therefore created in them a sense of desolation and insecurity. Guilt followed, and violence followed guilt. From this it was logical to conclude that the best interests of the Malagasy community would not be served by the granting of immediate political independence.

Mannoni's approach is in striking contrast to the one adopted by the British anthropologists M. Fortes and E. E. Evans-Pritchard in their *African Political Systems* (1940): "Most of these societies have been conquered or have submitted to European rule from fear of invasion. They would not acquiesce in it if the threat of force were withdrawn. . . ."[9] Fanon took his own lead from Césaire, who had attacked both Mannoni and the Belgian R. P. Tempels, who argued that the Bantu people had integrated the Belgians into their own hierarchical view of the world. Fanon insisted that whatever may have been the collective psychology of the Malagasies within their own closed community before colonization, it was irrelevant to an understanding of the attitudes they had adopted in a new, bilateral totality. With the coming of the conqueror, "the Malagasy has ceased to exist." The behavior patterns of a people confronted by superior, imperialist armed force were "not tacked on to a pre-existing set." Of course Mannoni had not said "tacked on," he had said "integrated into," and Fanon's suggestion of a complete psychological hiatus is unrealistic; on the other hand he was correct to emphasize that colonialism, far from being a collision between Crusoe and Man Friday, a benevolent paternalism, was in fact a form of systematic exploitation which created and perpetually reinforced a feeling of inferiority among the colonized

[9] M. Fortes and E. Evans-Pritchard (eds.), *African Political Systems* (New York, 1940).

people. So long as it endured, the whites would always regard the "natives" as things, as statistics, as faces bereft of humanity, as stray children who seemed to belong to nobody, as a kind of collective laziness sprawling in the sun. Fanon already believed that this imposed sense of inferiority could be exploded only by fighting back, by counterassertion, and in later years he attached increasing importance to the violent dimensions of decolonization.

"I do not carry innocence to the point of believing that appeals to reason or respect for human dignity can alter reality."[10] But this remark comes at the end of Fanon's first book, and within the general mood it is an afterthought. In *Black Skin, White Masks*, the young Fanon was still refining and polishing the bright jewel of universal reason which alone could release both oppressors and oppressed from their mutual mystification. His attention had been focused throughout on the educated Martinican, on the *évolué*, on himself: he had not yet become the champion of the "wretched of the earth." "The 'jungle savage' is not what I have in mind. That is because for him certain factors have not yet acquired importance."[11]

[10] Fanon, *Black Skin, White Masks*, p. 224.
[11] *Ibid.*, p. 14.

Negritude—the Black Mirage

● ●

11

"When you make men slaves you deprive them of half their virtue, you set them in your own conduct an example of fraud, rapine and cruelty . . . and yet you complain that they are not honest or faithful!"

So wrote an eighteenth-century former slave, Gustavus Vassa. The literature of black protest is as old and as varied in style as the history of modern slavery in its several national contexts. Protest and the voice of persuasion alternate with rage and cries of defiance. The key to Fanon's early thought lies in this tension between rage and reason, revolt and reconciliation.

Fanon's first debt was to Aimé Césaire, and particularly to his masterpieces *Cahier d'un retour au pays natal* and *Discours sur le colonialisme*. In Fanon's view, Césaire had virtually single-handed fostered the spirit of black pride in the people of the Antilles. "I wish that many black intellectuals would turn to him for inspiration." The *Cahier* is a long prose-poem which hurls tongues of fire and biting irony against the myth of a benevolent colonialism. Césaire evokes the life of the poor "brute beasts" who are good enough only to fertilize the "sweet sugar cane and the silky cotton," black men whose forebears were sold like cattle on the market square, toilers only now beginning to lift their heads and proclaim their solidarity with the universal oppressed: hyena-men, panther-men, Jew-men, Kaffir-men, Calcutta-Hindu-men, voteless men of Harlem, starving and insulted men, tortured men who could be broken with blows and killed without excuses or any explanation being rendered anywhere. "My race a ripe grape for drunken feet. . . ." It was the spirit of outrage and the spirit of revolt which Fanon searched for among the black poets, the mood conveyed in the direct, brutal lines of the young Senegalese poet David Diop: "The White Man killed my father/ My father was proud/ The White Man violated my mother/ My mother was beautiful. . . ."[1]

But Césaire represented more than black rage. His work was the quintessence of the whole ensemble of values, emotions, and historical perspectives known as "Negritude." This intricate ideology represented in its totality, in its cunning interplay of content and form, logic and feelings, in its claim to stand for the collective project of the black peoples, a central, problematical challenge to Fanon's discriminating intelligence.

Historically, the concept of Negritude derived from a number of related themes in the Caribbean litera-

[1] *Anthologie de la nouvelle poésie nègre et malgache* (Paris, 1948).

ture of the nineteenth and twentieth centuries. But more specifically it developed out of the Indigenist movement in the former French colony of Haiti, where the initial *prise de conscience* of the Negro living in a white world took place. One emerging theme was that of the forgotten richness of Negro-African history. Anténor Firmin's *De l'égalité des races humaines* (1885) anticipated several later works written on the high tide of the Negritude movement, especially Cheik Anta Diop's *Nations nègres et culture* (1956). The American occupation of Haiti, begun in 1915 and not relinquished until 1934, produced on the island a collective shock which resulted in a deliberate revival of African legends, proverbs, and music, and a concomitant rejection of European culture by black intellectuals who had been reared on it. These writers turned back to the countryside, to the peasants, and cultivated a spirit of reverence toward the most primitive aspects of local culture and folklore, including Voodoo.

It was not, however, in the Caribbean but rather in Paris, in the heart of the French *imperium*, that the specific literary movement associated with the concept of *négritude* took shape in the 1930s. Its three principal inspirers, all poets and all later politicians, were Césaire, Léopold Sédar Senghor of Senegal, and Léon Damas of French Guiana, whose bitter poems, *Pigments*, made an impact on Fanon. Caliban now rebels, breaking free from Prospero's *langage* (language as implicit ideology) by turning his professed values against himself and by breaking up the pattern of Prospero's *langue* (language as grammar). As Janheinz Jahn has pointed out,[2] Césaire's innovations were principally semantic, whereas Senghor's gentler poetry

[2] J. Jahn, *A History of Neo-African Literature.* Translated by O. Coburn and U. Lehrburger (London, 1968).

was distinguished more by its evocation of African rhythms. Negritude emerges as a literary style, a complex of racial attitudes, the affirmation of a Negro cultural essence, and as a possible instrument of liberation.

But here a paradox and a limitation becomes apparent. For, distinctive as the stylistic innovations of the black poets undoubtedly were, these innovations were strongly influenced by trends in contemporary French poetry. Césaire and Étienne Lero in particular owed a good deal to the work of left-wing surrealists such as André Breton and, by earlier derivation, to Rimbaud, Baudelaire, and Lautréamont. Except by implication, analogy, or suggestive posture, surrealism was not, despite Breton's protestations to the contrary, an effective vehicle or mode for social and racial revolution. Its emphasis on spontaneity and the subconscious, as well as its involvement with metaphysics and the irrational, linked it to bohemian revolt rather than to any historically concrete theory of social change. Sartre hailed black poetry in the French language as the only great revolutionary poetry of the time, but he recognized its limitations as he had recognized those of Breton's surrealism. He described Césaire's poetry as destructive, free, metaphysical, a cry of grief, hatred, and love; but it was at the same time a poetry which only a small coterie of French-speaking intellectuals could understand or appreciate.

In 1948 there appeared in Paris an excellent anthology of new black poetry, edited by Senghor and with a preface by Sartre. The mood or movement of Negritude dominated the volume. But particularly significant was the fact that, leaving aside the Malagasies, only three of the poets included came from Africa. The others came from Guiana (Damas), Martinique (Gratiant, Lero, Césaire), Guadeloupe (Tirolien, Niger), and Haiti (Laleau, Roumain, Brière, Belance). Thus we see in an instant that the appeal and inspiration of Negritude was almost exclusively limited to the most "advanced" and assimilated far west of the French Empire, to those regions where the sense of uprootedness created a combination of nostalgia for African primitivism, political radicalism, and intellectual sophistication. The three African poets included in the volume, Birago Diop, David Diop, and Senghor himself, all came from the most advanced and assimilated area of French West Africa, Senegal. These poets entered into a voluntary exile which induced a psycho-cultural-racial outlook similar to that of the West Indians. Negritude was almost wholly divorced from the great continent of Africa. If for this reason alone, its pretentions to lead the mass of black "brute beasts" to freedom were stillborn.

What is more, the notion of Negritude, for all its outward ferocity, yields a small but vital concession to the prevailing white culture. The white man, master of the world, never bothered to create a literary ideology around his whiteness. As the Nigerian poet Wole Soyinka remarked, why should a tiger need to proclaim his "tigritude"? Men like Senghor and Césaire had mortgaged a portion of their hearts and minds to white culture. There is a direct line of continuity between Senghor's poem *Luxembourg* (1939), in which he calls himself a "cultural mulatto," and his blatantly Francophile policy as President of Senegal twenty years later. As for Césaire, we shall see presently how he received André Malraux when de Gaulle's spokesman arrived in Martinique in 1958.

About much of this Fanon gradually became aware by a constant process of distillation and crossexamination. In the first instance, he was both attracted to and alienated by Césaire's celebration of Negro primitivism. "And it is not only the mouths which sing, but the hands, but the feet, but the bottoms, but the sexes, and the entire creature which liquefies into sound, voice and rhythm." Who and what are we?, asks Césaire in his poem. "Admirable question! By dint of watching the trees I have become a tree . . . by dint of thinking of the Congo, I have become a Congo roaring with forests and rivers . . . where the water goes likoula-likoula. . . ." Fanon found himself swept along by this exhilarating Congo and by Césaire's defiant rejection of the white man's technical and military prowess:

Eia for those who have never invented anything
for those who have never explored anything
for those who have never subjugated anything.[3]

For these are the blacks "without whom the earth would not be the earth," the toilers whose Negritude "thrusts into the red flesh of the sun." Fanon quotes Senghor's vision of the Negro as an essentially emotional man whose roots are deep in the earth, a man who joins himself cosmically to the world, whereas the European divorces himself from nature in order to master and subdue it. Then abruptly Fanon's rationality asserts itself; the dream is over. "Nevertheless," he writes, "one had to distrust rhythm, earth-mother love, this mystic, carnal marriage of the group and the cosmos."[4]

Fanon had, figuratively, stood before a mirror, trying on the bright-colored garments of black primitivism and black history for size and discarding them one by one. He experimented by dancing naked before the white man, spear in hand, but the white man was not impressed. "I jostled him and told him point-blank,

[3] A. Césaire, *Cahier d'un retour au pays natal* (Paris, 1956).
[4] Fanon, *Black Skin, White Masks* (New York, 1967), p. 125.

'Get used to me, I am not getting used to anyone.' "
But the white man informed him that the serious business in the world was the matter of mastering it. So,
said Fanon, "Every hand was a losing hand for me."
His final verdict is clear: "In no way should I derive
my basic purpose from the people of color. In no way
should I dedicate myself to the revival of an unjustly
unrecognized Negro civilization."[5] Marx, after all, had
insisted that "the social revolution . . . cannot draw its
poetry from the past, but only from the future. It cannot begin with itself before it has stripped itself of all
superstitions concerning the past." Fanon added words
of his own: "Those Negroes and white men will be dis-
alienated who refuse to let themselves be sealed away
in the materialized Tower of the Past."

It is clear that the young Fanon was determined to
cut his way through the veils of prejudice and irra-
tionality, and, through his own humiliating experiences, toward a universal reason. Here, again, the influence of Sartre is evident. In his essay *Orphée Noir*
(1948), Sartre had argued that the subjective, existential, ethnic idea of Negritude passes, in the Hegelian
sense, into the objective, positive, exact idea of the
proletariat. The affirmation of white supremacy provides the thesis; Negritude as an authentic value was
the moment of negativity; the creation of a humanity
without "races" would be the synthesis. Negritude is
thereby viewed as the minor term of a dialectical progression. Fanon commented, "When I read that page I
felt that I had been robbed of my last chance. . . ."
Fanon attempted to retaliate. Sartre, he wrote, "had
forgotten that consciousness has to lose itself in the
night of the absolute. . . . A consciousness committed

[5] *Ibid.*, p. 226.

to experience is ignorant, has to be ignorant, of the essences and determinations of its being."[6] But this won't do. Fanon is precisely one of those intellectuals whose "commitment to experience" is constantly harried by their externalized overview of themselves. Sartre's argument struck home, as is seen in Fanon's later (1955) reflection that in Martinique the birth of proletarian politics coincided with the birth of black awareness. Césaire himself had made common cause with the French Communists and was calling (somewhat rhetorically, it is true) for a proletarian revolution in Europe.

Of course, when we consider Fanon's later total disenchantment with both the white, metropolitan proletariat and the nascent working class of the colonies—a developing perspective largely shared by Sartre—these dialectical speculations may resemble colored balloons drifting to and fro between Europe and the Caribbean. It is one of the smaller ironies of intellectual history that both Sartre and Fanon, in their progress from a form of socialist humanism to a tougher, neo-Marxist doctrine of violent revolution, jettisoned the proletariat in the course of the passage.

Sartre is fine, but Fanon remains black. When Fanon closes the pages of Sartre, determined to follow the master and rise above his own transitory Negritude, he must still face a white world where his medical degree counts for less than his skin. It is Fanon, not Sartre, whom people will continue to address as "*tu.*" Here the black intellectual's predicament resembles that of Bigger Thomas, the hero of Richard Wright's novel *Native Son*, which Fanon admired. The greatest threat in the Chicago slum kid Bigger's life arises when two white people, a rich girl and her Communist friend,

[6] *Ibid.*, p. 134.

try to befriend him, to treat him as an equal. Their generosity threatens the identity which white society has thrust on him and endangers his defensive reflexes without in any way insuring him against the vengeance of that society. Bigger half-unintentionally murders the girl, burns her body, and embarks upon a dim, twilight odyssey of existential self-discovery among the derelict buildings of Chicago's South Side. "Confidence could only come again now through action so violent that it would make him forget."[7] The young Fanon appears to face this option, only to step back—as a doctor of medicine well might.

In 1956 both Fanon and Richard Wright were present at the First Congress of Black Writers and Artists in Paris. Wright made a short intervention to the effect that in his opinion the ultimate result of European intervention in Africa had been to liberate the Africans from an irrational past and to introduce them to the blessings of the Enlightenment. Hardly a speech to evoke applause from Fanon! But this incident draws attention to a dilemma about the formation of a single, black consciousness which extends beyond the specific question of Negritude. In 1947 the review *Présence Africaine* had been founded in Paris. It was edited by Alioune Diop and officially patronized by a distinguished galaxy of liberal and left-wing Frenchmen, including Gide, Camus, Rivet, Mounier, Sartre, Naville, and Leiris. This review exerted a formative influence on Fanon: he quotes from it extensively in *Black Skin, White Masks* and attributes to it his ability to coordinate the psychological motivation governing men of color. What the contents of *Présence Africaine* unwittingly masked, and what the Paris Congress brought into

[7] R. Wright, *Native Son* (New York, 1940).

the open, was the wide gulf in attitudes separating "French" from "British" Negroes, and both from the Americans. "I am a Frenchman," Fanon had written. "I am interested in French culture, French civilization, the French people. We [the blacks] refuse to be considered 'outsiders'; we have full part in the French drama."[8] And this involved not only the rejection of Negritude, it meant to any Francophone integration with the most universal of all cultures. Now, in 1956, Fanon came face to face with the division of the Negroes into their different European particularisms, a division which thereafter led him to regard the Negro's culture, like the white man's, as first and foremost national. Senghor, who told the congress that the British and American Negroes were pragmatists, whereas the French were Cartesians, concluded, "That's why, quite often, you don't follow us, as we don't follow you. . . ." James Baldwin's account of the congress,[9] in terms of his own reactions to the rhetoric of Senghor and Césaire, and in terms of his description of the short shrift given the Bible-clutching black "Anglo-Saxons" by the black French rationalists, indicates that Senghor's allusion to mutual noncomprehension was not wide of the mark. One might as well ask a French Socialist deputy to understand why British Labour M. P.s spend their Sunday mornings in church. Among African leaders of "British" descent, Jomo Kenyatta, Julius K. Nyerere, Kenneth D. Kaunda, and Kwame Nkrumah have all declared themselves to be Christians. When Fanon arrived in Accra, Ghana, in 1960, as Ambassador of the Algerian Provisional Government, he found himself partly out of sympathy with a culture

---

[8] Fanon, *Black Skin, White Masks*, p. 203.
[9] J. Baldwin, "Princes and Powers," *Nobody Knows My Name* (New York, 1954).

very different from his own. On the other hand, it is obvious that in the United States today Christianity is increasingly associated by the black intelligentsia with meekness and integration; hence the drive toward either a black, Muslim religion or, alternatively, toward a neo-Marxist atheism.

But if the Negroes who attended the Paris Congress found themselves divided, Fanon was never tempted to revert to Negritude as a solution to the fragmentation of the black world. He did not agree with Senghor that African culture and African history provided viable living ideologies. "To believe that it is possible to create a black culture," he wrote in 1961, "is to forget that niggers are disappearing, just as those people who brought them into being are seeing the breakup of their economic and cultural supremacy."[10] He regarded Senghor's introduction of Negritude as a subject of study in the Senegalese schools as a retrograde step.

In *The Wretched of the Earth*, Fanon analyzes the development of black writing in the colonies in terms of a three-stage evolution. First, there is a general attempt to assimilate the occupying culture; black writers involve themselves to the extent of imitating and championing, for example, the French symbolist and surrealist poets. Then comes a phase of withdrawal and a search for an authentic local identity. But the black writer, says Fanon, finds himself cut off from his own people by his European culture, with the result that he relies on legends and pays exaggerated attention to the exotic aspects of folklore and festival. The final phase arrives with the emergence of a fighting, revolutionary literature; here the writer "goes to the people," learns from them, inspires them, and identifies totally with

[10] Fanon, *The Wretched of the Earth* (New York, 1965), p. 188.

their struggle. (Mao, of course, had called for such a literature at the Yenan Forum.) Fanon cited and quoted Keita Fodeba's poem *Aube Africaine* (*African Dawn*) as an excellent example of revolutionary demystification.

This scheme follows closely that of Sartre; Negritude represents the second, intermediary phase, the phase of negation which in turn produces its own *dépassement*. And behind Sartre lies the dialectical thought of Marx and Hegel. Clearly "triadic" interpretations have an enduring appeal to the human mind, but what is particularly noticeable in the case of Fanon is how his West Indian background and his rationalist-essentialist philosophical heritage result in an abstract overview which ignores the variables of African development. For one thing, the Martinican in him ignores the complicating impact of local African languages, both oral and written. As Jahn has pointed out, "apprentice" literature (respectful toward the colonizers) does not always involve assimilation of the occupying culture and language. Southern Bantu "apprentice" literature was generally expressed in local languages based on an oral tradition of storytelling. Conversely, a good deal of early "protest" literature was articulated in European languages. Again, an African writer such as Ephraim Amu of the Gold Coast could rally his countrymen against the invader in his native Turi, an option not available to the writers of the Caribbean, who were at that time engaged in both perfecting and fragmenting the French language in the service of a somewhat artificial and exotic ideology of Negritude. In certain respects Fanon remained a stranger to the realities of the continent whose freedom he so ardently championed.

A Philosophy in Transition

● ● ●

iii

The form a book takes tells us something about its content. The pages of *Black Skin, White Masks* are heavy with scholarly references and footnotes; in *The Wretched of the Earth* they are few and far between. Although the first book is brought to vibrant life by the intensity of the author's own experiences, these experiences are carefully interpreted with reference to numerous philosophers, psychologists, linguists, and anthropologists. The young Fanon, a deeply committed and programmatic writer, was also an emerging intellectual flexing his academic muscles; he calls *Black Skin, White Masks* "a clinical study." In the last book it is life itself, the world groaning in upheaval, that sweeps the narrative along.

There would be no point in making a complete list of the authorities and sources whom

Fanon invokes, and sometimes castigates, in his first book. Hegel is there, and Marx, Nietzsche, and Valéry, Jaspers and Marcel, Lacan, Piaget, Mounier and Leiris, Gide and Duhamel, as well as Sartre and Merleau-Ponty (whose lectures Fanon attended at Lyons). As for the psychoanalysts, Fanon's range is catholic almost to the point of eclecticism. Freud, Jung, and Adler, Leconte and Damey, Anna Freud, Helene Deutsch, and Marie Bonaparte all receive close attention. In his later work he discarded much of this intellectual scaffolding; he no longer *interpreted* social philosophy, he *made* it.

The evolution of Fanon's thought parallels in certain respects that of Marx and, more closely, that of Sartre. The early (pre-1845) Marx, like the early Fanon, tended to treat "man" as an anthropological abstraction. In the *Economic and Philosophic Manuscripts*, Marx writes of "man's essential powers," the "natural essence of man," and "true anthropological nature." Fanon writes, "All forms of exploitation are identical because all of them are applied against the same 'object': man." To forget this, he says, is when "one simply turns one's back on the major basic problem, which is that of restoring man to his proper place."[1] Fanon's "proper place" is the humanistic equivalent of Marx's "true anthropological nature." Although the young Marx was already a materialist who analyzed the human predicament as a social predicament, he was inclined to equate human alienation with self-alienation. Fanon strikes this note when he writes, "I seriously hope to persuade my brother, whether black or white, to tear off with all his strength the shameful livery put together by centuries of incomprehension."[2] Here

[1] Fanon, *Black Skin, White Masks* (New York, 1967), p. 88.
[2] *Ibid.*, p. 14.

"incomprehension" can be taken in the same sense as "mystification" and "false consciousness" in the work of Marx.

Of course, the notion that all forms of exploitation are identical is vulnerable to formal logical objections. Are all forms of physical pain deliberately inflicted on man identical because it is on man that they are inflicted? But it was not by posing such questions that Fanon transcended his early tendency toward anthropological abstraction.

In both Marx and Fanon there is a progression from humanism to sociology. The original themes are not so much discarded as posed on a new, more concrete level. The re-emergence of universal reason is seen to require profound historical and social changes. Aimé Césaire, in a posthumous tribute to Fanon, remarked that *Black Skin, White Masks* was the crucial book on the human consequences of colonization and racism, while *The Wretched of the Earth* provided the key to the process of decolonization. In Fanon's first work, "liberation" rather than "revolution" is the typical notion; nowhere is there any mention of socialism. Put in different terms, we can speak of three successive Fanons: the de-alienated man (*Black Skin, White Masks*), the free citizen of Algeria (*Studies in a Dying Colonialism*), and the socialist revolutionary (*The Wretched of the Earth*). R. D. Laing has written, "The task of social phenomenology is to relate my experience of the other's behavior to the other's experience of my behavior."[3] This is precisely what Fanon was attempting in his early work. In the later writings, however, the descriptive emphasis of phenomenology gives way to a study of the dialectics of revolution; Fanon was now

[3] R. D. Laing, *The Politics of Experience* (New York, 1967).

concerned to overthrow by force the tyrannical Other so that the colonized Self might achieve freedom and authentic individuality in the process. (Marx: "The philosophers have only *interpreted* the world differently, the point is, to *change* it.") The *"coupure"* in Marx's work came in 1845-1846; for Fanon the crucial years of reformulation were 1954-1956. Just as the later Marx roots alienation firmly in the division of labor and in class struggle, the later Fanon locates it equally firmly in the imperialist division of the world into poor countries and rich, exploiters and exploited, rulers and ruled. For the young Marx, the industrial proletariat typifies the condition of being socially exploited in its most radical form; for the young Fanon, the colonized blacks occupy this position. Like the later Marx, the later Fanon transforms the ultra-exploited into a universal class whose historical mission it is to overthrow by violence the social conditions which engender exploitation. This class, when brought to the correct ideological consciousness of its own situation and collective project, becomes the embodiment of historical truth. "Now, the *fellah*, the unemployed man, the starving native do not lay a claim to the truth: they do not *say* that they represent the truth, for they *are* the truth."[4]

Fanon began his studies in France in the postwar years when the impact of Sartre's teaching as philosopher, novelist, playwright, and socialist was reaching its peak. Fanon's debt to Sartre is beyond question, and it was Sartre's close disciple, Francis Jeanson, who wrote the preface to the original French edition of *Black Skin, White Masks*. Fanon's prose reverberates with Sartrian concepts, phrases, dialectical juxtapositions, paradoxes, and essentialist abstractions. In his

[4] Fanon, *The Wretched of the Earth* (New York, 1965), p. 38.

monumental work on Jean Genet, Sartre argued that bourgeois society had made Genet the thief and homosexual that he was. "They took a child and made a monster of him for reasons of social utility." The lesson for the Negro was not obscure; did not the same logic apply to Bigger Thomas?

But Fanon was not a philosopher—he was a social philosopher. A philosopher such as Sartre makes a rigorous exploration of *method*; what is "recognition" in the social philosopher is also "cognition" in the philosopher. Fanon's methodology is mainly implicit (and this became increasingly true in his later work) whereas Sartre's is explicit. At the same time it has to be said that a Negro is "thrown into the world" in a total sense which escapes the white man, and therefore the testimony of a Fanon provides indispensable evidence for the wider and more complexly articulated system of a Sartre. In terms of social philosophy, Fanon made approximately the same journey from *Black Skin, White Masks* to *The Wretched of the Earth* that Sartre made from *Being and Nothingness* to the *Critique of Dialectical Reason*. The major distinction lies in the fact that the two works of Sartre embody fundamental explorations of philosophical method. It is also the case that their publication preceded and strongly influenced the respective books by Fanon. In both writers there is a visible retreat from the existentialist emphasis on individual freedom of choice, and therefore on the availability of a universal reason, accompanied by a growing attention to social determination. Sartre finally proclaimed himself a Marxist, relegating existentialism to the status of a marginal subphilosophy which would vanish once its insights into individual behavior had been fully incorporated into a Marxism which, in the hands of its contemporary practitioners, tended to be "an inhuman anthropology." Fanon also sustained his interest in the microcosmic units of society. The Vietnamese Communist Nguyen Nghe noticed and complained about the retention of existentialist traits in Fanon's later work, dismissing them as "vestiges of subjectivism." The accusation was particularly pointed at Fanon's theory of violence.

This general evolution within Fanon's thought is further clarified by his published reflections on psychoanalysis and psychiatry.

The traditional hostility between Freudian psychoanalysis and Marxism, or between Sartrian existentialism and the School of Freud, is well known. Whereas the "natural sciences" tend to be divided and defined by the different areas of matter and life they study, the "social sciences" frequently resemble rival armies competing to establish a monopoly of interpretation over the same reserve. Here, for example, is Stokely Carmichael addressing the Dialectics of Liberation congress held in London in July 1967: ". . . I'm not a psychologist or a psychiatrist, I'm a political activist and I don't deal with the individual. I think it's a cop out when people talk about the individual. . . . I want to talk about the system."[5] Curiously enough, he goes on to support this view by quoting from his "patron saint," Frantz Fanon. But he evidently misunderstands what he is quoting. To say, as Fanon does, that "the black man's alienation is not an individual question," is by no means to infer that it is a "cop out" to talk about the individual. Social philosophers who take this hard line, and who deal exclusively in terms of macrosmic social categories and systems, often fall precisely into the "inhuman anthropology" about which Sartre com-

[5] D. Cooper, ed., *The Dialectics of Liberation* (London, 1968).

plained. It is one of Fanon's great virtues as a writer that he constantly relates the psychological predicament of the individual to his environment without losing sight of the individual.

Fanon's view was that the Negro's inferiority complex was mainly economic in its origins; subsequently the black man internalized and epidermalized this economic inferiority. He criticized Freud for his undue emphasis on the "ontogenetic," and insisted that the only useful approach to the psychology of groups was a socio-diagnostic one. Despite his critical attitude toward Freud, Adler, and Jung, he fully appreciated the value of their insights into repression, sublimation, and compensation, harnessing into his own synthesis Freud's work on childhood sexuality and, with severe reservations, Jung's theory of the collective unconscious.

Only a psychoanalytical interpretation of the black problem, said Fanon, could lay bare the anomalies of affect that are responsible for the complex. "The neurotic structure of an individual is simply the elaboration, the formation, the eruption within the ego, of conflictual clusters arising in part out of the environment and in part out of the purely personal way in which the individual reacts to these influences."[6] But this is description, and the main problem is one of causation, of genesis. Fanon in fact attempted to synthesize or reconcile causal traditions which are often regarded as mutually alien: social and economic determination, "psychological" determination, and the existentialist emphasis on freedom of self-determination. The difficulty of reconciling these traditions is particularly apparent in his discussion of sexual neuroses in the context of race.

He accepted Pierre Naville's argument that sexuality

[6] Fanon, *Black Skin, White Masks,* p. 81.

and dreams are given shape by the individual's socio-economic situation, but he related this principle more fluently to the black sexual drive toward the white than to white sexual phobias toward the black. On the one side, there is the desire for possession of, integration with, and recognition by the dominant culture. But, says Fanon, all Negrophobic women have had abnormal sex lives; they all imaginatively endow Negroes with powers that they have been deprived of and fear. The Negrophobic man suffers from a sense of sexual inferiority and then projects his own hidden desires onto the Negro. But here Fanon is reluctant to commit himself to a general explanation. He hints that "civilization" itself creates such neuroses, and adds that "every intellectual gain requires a loss in sexual potential." In general he sees the black sexual drive toward the white as the consequence of "the unreflected imposition of a culture," whereas the black man enters the neurotic structure of particular white people in a symbolic role determined by his social and biological associations.

After 1954 Fanon was increasingly inclined to concentrate on the socio-economic causes of mental stress. He consistently attacked the misuse of psychiatric techniques to adapt alienated men to an alienating environment—hence his criticism of American psychotherapists who set about adjusting workers to bad factory conditions by stimulating a symbolic identification with unreal roles. In an article published in February 1952,[7] he drew attention to the difficulties of giving medical treatment to North Africans living in France. Often the behavior of the Arab patients made French doctors impatient and distrustful about the reality of their illness. The patients tended to give vague and

[7] Fanon, "Le 'syndrome nord-africain,'" *Pour la révolution africaine* (Paris, 1964).

unhelpful replies, to be confused about the precise lo-
cation of their pain, and to identify totally with the
pain. Well, *"tout Arabe est un malade imaginaire."*
What the white doctors failed to understand was the
psychic effect on the Arabs of living in an unfamiliar
environment, cut off from family and friends, faced
with perpetual insecurity, a kind of living death. It was
for these reasons that an apparently healthy and physi-
cally robust Arab would swear passionately to the doctor that he was going to die. For these men expatria-
tion was in itself a morbid phenomenon.

Fanon's belief that the first condition of mental
health is social health is seen again in his letter of
resignation sent to the Resident Minister of Algeria,
Lacoste, in 1956. Fanon had been *"Chef de Service"* in
the psychiatric hospital of Blida-Joinville since October
1953, but for two years the Algerian revolution had
been gathering momentum and now he had reached his
decisive moment, the moment of rupture from France.
In his letter, he pointed out that psychiatry is a medical
technique for preventing man from feeling a stranger to
his environment. But official French policy insured
precisely that every Algerian Arab would feel alienated
in his own country, reduced to a state of "absolute depersonalization," the victim of an abortive attempt, as
Fanon put it, to decerebralize a whole people. It was
no use for Frenchmen to lament, much less to hope to
cure, the antisocial habits of the Arab—his tendency to
reach for his knife, to kill for small causes—so long
as the Arab lived in the midst of famine, malnutrition,
unemployment, insecurity, and frustration. He re-
called how, as a young soldier waiting to board a ship
at Oran in 1944, he had watched the troops throwing
bits of bread to Arab children; the children fought
furiously for the bread in a welter of anger, hatred,

and violence, thus learning the law of the farmyard which society would never let them forget.

Negro-African society was saturated with apparently aberrant practices and rituals which the whites contemptuously attributed to innate psychic instability. The blacks believed in leopardmen, serpentmen, six-legged dogs, zombies, juju, witchcraft, and the rest. According to Fanon, these myths and rites fulfilled well-defined functions in the dynamism of the collective libido. Under certain oppressive conditions, the psyche shrinks back and finds outlet in muscular exertions, the communal effort of a society to exorcise, liberate, and define itself. But during the liberation struggle, he said, these habits were noticeably discarded. If, as seems to be the case, Fanon attributed tribal magic and rituals exclusively to the effects of colonial rule, then he was mistaken. These rituals were altered and sometimes inflamed by white domination. The Mau Mau rebellion against the British settlers among the Kikuyu of Kenya was accompanied by an intensification of violent rituals. But it should be stressed that harsh British military repression succeeded precisely in preventing the emergence of a coordinated national liberation movement, and drove the armed peasants back into the tactical and ideological preformations of a Jacquerie, back into myth and magic.

From the time of his resignation from Blida-Joinville Hospital in 1956 until his death five years later, Fanon continued to pay close attention to individual cases of psychiatric disorder. But the emphasis changes in accordance with the general evolution of his thought. In *Black Skin, White Masks*, the experience of the individual is the starting point, the area of primary reference, while colonial and general sociological determinants are introduced by way of background and explanation.

In the later work, the focus is on the political and racial struggle, with specific case-histories of nervous disorder introduced by way of illustration. The academic apparatus and the references to major authorities disappear. The young Fanon was a professional psychiatrist with strong political and racial convictions; the mature Fanon was a revolutionary whose perception of the human consequences of collective violence was enriched by his knowledge of psychiatry.

Algeria

•

IV

In the space of a few years the Fourth French
Republic had been compelled to abandon its
Colonial possessions in Indochina, Tunisia, and
Morocco. The French Army was deeply humiliated by its defeat at Dien Bien Phu, and its
officer corps was determined to halt the retreat.
Algeria was the natural place. Algeria had belonged to France since 1830, and it was colonized in depth. Quite apart from France's exten-
sive economic stake in the country, including
the oil of the Sahara, over a million *"colons,"* or
"pieds-noirs," of European descent lived, worked,
and farmed the soil in Algeria. Algeria was regarded as indissolubly "part of France."

The rebellion began in 1954. Pierre Mendès-
France, Premier at the time, declared that it
would be crushed. The left-wing election victory
of 1956 promised some hope of compromise or

concession, but early in 1957 the Socialist Premier Guy Mollet capitulated to the pressure of the *Algérie française* ultras, and thereafter the scene was set for total war; for violence, hatred, killing, and torture which spread from Algeria to France itself, decimated the Algerian people, brought down the Fourth Republic, and raised the specter of military rule or fascism in France.

In this way Fanon learned about violence. His commentaries on the war are contained in two volumes of collected essays, *Studies in a Dying Colonialism* and *For the African Revolution*.

By January 1957, the Resident Minister, René Lacoste, to whom Fanon had sent his letter of resignation, had handed over all police and security operations in Algiers to General Jacques Massu's Tenth Parachute Regiment. The "paras" employed hooded informers who pointed out National Liberation Front (FLN) sympathizers as they streamed out to work from the precincts of the Casbah. These and other methods of repression proved effective. Urban terrorism was stamped out. The FLN withdrew to the countryside and concentrated on guerrilla warfare. Out of this development grew the central thesis of *The Wretched of the Earth*.

Fanon remarks ironically that the French soon discovered that the rebellion was inspired and financed from abroad, particularly from Nasser's Egypt and from Moscow. Even Albert Camus spoke in 1958 of not abandoning Algeria to a new imperialism. The FLN, he said, intended the eviction of 1.2 million Europeans and the humiliation of millions of Frenchmen. Compared to the opinions of the professional officers serving in Algeria, Camus' position was a mild one. They, or many of them, believed they were engaged in a holy war, one further encounter against a malevolent, universal, materialist conspiracy to destroy Western civilization. Their "pacification" tactics were as totalitarian as their ideology. First, as Fanon says, they tried to divide the so-called "sane" or loyal population from the rebels, a strategy to which the United States continues to adhere in Vietnam. They also promised far-reaching economic and social reforms, and indeed some of them were sincere about this, but it was a lobby of French-Algerian industrialists who controlled Algerian economic policy, not the officers. The Army also attempted with some success to exploit rivalry between the FLN and the MNA, the "Messalistes." Massacres were staged and then attributed to the FLN. Fanon cites the killings at Mélouza and Wagram as the worst examples. (At Mélouza, about three hundred males over the age of fifteen were slaughtered. In fact this village was an MNA stronghold, and not only the French but also the MNA blamed the FLN.) Next, whole populations were deported in order to cut them off from the guerrillas of the National Liberation Army, the military arm of the FLN; by 1959, about two million Arabs, almost a quarter of the total population, had been forced to leave their villages to prevent contamination and intimidation by the guerrillas, who were, in fact, their own fathers, sons, brothers, and husbands. Meanwhile frustration and fear among the French led to frequent indiscriminate *"ratissages,"* killer raids on villages suspected of harboring guerrillas, or, indeed, simply suspected of being populated by Algerians. The fascistic violence of white territorial units was notorious.

In the urban police stations and military detention centers a new breed of torturers came up from the sewers like the rats in Camus' novel about Oran, *The Plague*. The majority of victims were Arabs, but Europeans who worked for Algerian independence were not immune. Maurice Audin, a twenty-five-year-old French professor of mathematics at the Algiers Faculty of Science, was strangled by paratroopers in the course of a torture session at El Biar. Another French Communist resident in Algeria, Henri Alleg, provided a terrible testimony to his own sufferings in his book *The Question* (1958). No one was immune. The security forces burned off the tongue of Mohamed Sefta, Registrar of the Mahakma (Moslem Court) of Algiers. A young girl, Djamila Boupacha, accused of planting a bomb in a university restaurant, was pumped full of soapy water and violated with a glass bottle. Her seventy-one-year-old father was given electric shocks while his torturers explained to him, "No humanity for Arabs." Algerian students living in Paris were meanwhile being rounded up, taken to the rue des Saussaies and other police stations, and hideously tortured. Few lawyers could be found to act on behalf of the victims, and those who did were harassed and intimidated. The Army High Command and the Minister of War in Paris blocked all efforts at investigation. As for the occasional Commissions of Inquiry set up by the French Government, they had no meaning for the Arabs. After seven years of atrocities, not a single Frenchman had been convicted before a French court for the murder of an Algerian.

Fanon noted this. We begin to see why and how the "early" Fanon became the "late" Fanon.

The basic ethics of medicine which Fanon had learned in France and which he had believed all French doctors would respect were being disregarded on a massive scale. For where, in the rage of a colonial war, does "civilization" make its values felt? Simone de Beauvoir and the Tunisian lawyer Gisèle Halimi confirm Fanon's evidence that French doctors took part in torture sessions and later denied all knowledge of the practice of torture. Henri Alleg supports Fanon's charge that some doctors administered the "truth serum," which has hypnotic qualities but is liable to impair permanently the personality of the victim. Doctors were employed to revive prisoners, while psychiatrists helped to administer shock treatment. "When I search for Man in the technique and the style of Europe, I see only a succession of negations of man, and an avalanche of murders."[1]

Fanon refers to a number of case-histories to illustrate the nervous and mental effects of torture on both violators and victims. A European police inspector, who was deeply involved in torture sessions, became increasingly autocratic and violent in all his relationships, until he found himself beating his own wife and children. At this point he came to the hospital for help and was put under Fanon's care. "He asked me without beating about the bush to help him go on torturing Algerian patriots without any prickings of conscience, without any behavior problems and with complete equanimity."[2] In his preface to Alleg's *The Question*, Sartre remarks, "It is the executioner who becomes *Sisyphus*. If he puts the question at all, he will have to continue forever."

In Fanon's view, the different morbidity groups that came to his notice or under his care corresponded to the different methods of torture employed (although it must be said that he asserts rather than proves this simple correlation). Those who had been the victims of "indiscriminate" techniques, such as the high-pressure injection of an enema and soapy water down the throat,

[1] Fanon, *The Wretched of the Earth* (New York, 1965), p. 252.
[2] *Ibid.*, p. 217.

formed one group, the victims of electric torture, another. Anal penetration with a bottle was a familiar method, as was "motionless" torture (the suspect is beaten every time he moves). Fanon makes the interesting claim that those patriots who had really harbored information never subsequently became hospital patients; traumas and mental disorders were confined to those who had had no information to hide. Fanon ultimately doubted whether the primary motivation of torture in Algeria was to gain information; it was better explained as a symptom of sadistic racist fury. It was a fundamental necessity of the colonialist world.

Césaire, and with him Fanon, had likened colonialism to Hitlerism. Very often men put down the truth before they fully believe it. Fanon knew that the French in Algeria were merely reproducing and adapting to local conditions techniques they had already employed in Indochina and which the British had resorted to in Kenya. (By 1955, there were forty-eight thousand Africans detained without trial in Kenya. Duncan McPherson, an Assistant Commissioner of Police, testified that he found some detention camps worse than anything he had experienced during his four and a half years as a prisoner of the Japanese.[3] Systematic beatings, tortures and mutilations culminated with the "scandal" of eleven men being beaten to death at Hola Camp in 1959.) To Fanon, every "scandal," every "case" which shook Paris or London, was symptomatic of the refusal of the European intellectuals to diagnose colonialism for what it was.

But were there not many Europeans of good will in Algeria—democrats, radicals, friends of the Algerian people?

[3] *Gangrene.* Introduction by P. Benenson (London, 1959).

After 1956 Fanon worked in Tunis for the free Algerian press service and for the FLN paper, *El Moudjahid*. Therefore it has to be stressed that the majority of articles that he wrote during the war were specifically addressed to Algerians by an adopted Algerian. Writing in December 1957, he justified the FLN ambush and massacre of ten civilians at Sakamody on the grounds that under colonial rule "the Frenchman in Algeria cannot be neutral or innocent. Every Frenchman in Algeria oppresses, despises, dominates. . . . Every Frenchman in Algeria is in reality an enemy soldier. So long as Algeria is not independent, one must accept this logical consequence. . . ." Thrusting salt into the wound, he added, "Every Frenchman in Algeria has to behave like a torturer."[4] Fanon's position here, with a predominantly Algerian audience in his sights, strongly contrasts with an article he published in Sartre's Paris magazine, *Les Temps Modernes*, in June 1959. "It has often been claimed that the FLN made no distinction among the different members of Algeria's European society. Those who make such accusations fail to take into account both the policy long defined by the Front with respect to Algeria's Europeans, and the constant support that hundreds and hundreds of European men and women have brought to our units and to our political cells."[5] Many European doctors had given help to the maquis units of the National Liberation Army, highly placed civil servants had furnished the required false documents to FLN cells, and ordinary farmers had allowed guerrilla commandos to store arms and supplies in their granaries. (Here Fanon

[4] Fanon, *Pour la révolution africaine* (Paris, 1964), pp. 90 and 78.
[5] Fanon, *Studies in a Dying Colonialism* (New York, 1965), p. 149.

simply ignores the factor of intimidation.) He re-emphasized the point in *The Wretched of the Earth*: "The barriers of blood and race-prejudice are broken down on both sides." But this was the dilemma. Taking the colonial situation in its objective totality as foreign military rule, the subjugated people could not afford to make distinctions, to be disarmed by occasional white altruism or heroism, to falter in their stride. So long as the war continued, every Arab was a Bigger Thomas.

But what of the French Left, the spirit of 1789, the great radical-Jacobin tradition? The elections of 1956 had, after all, resulted in a victory for a left-wing coalition pledged to bring peace to Algeria. The answer is short: the Left betrayed its pledge. Fanon's scorn raked the Socialist Party, the Radicals, and the left MRP, whose combined forces contained hardly a single voice sympathetic to Algerian independence. As for the local branches of these parties in Algeria, said Fanon, they contented themselves with parroting the slogans of the metropolitan parties, consistently ignoring that the issue was first and last one of *national independence*. But could the same strictures be leveled at the Communist Party, supported by more than five million proletarian and peasant voters and dedicated to the intransigently anti-imperialist heritage of Marx and Lenin?

In May 1945, riots had broken out in the Constantine department of Algeria. The Communist Party had called for the punishment of the instigators and had set its face firmly against Algerian independence. But then attention switched to Indochina, and from 1949 the Communist Party was to be found in the forefront of opposition to the war against Ho Chi Minh and the Vietminh. The Party leader Maurice Thorez saluted the French dockers who refused to load arms bound for

Indochina, while railway sabotage was actively encouraged. Ho sent messages of gratitude and appreciation: the Leninist alliance of the metropolitan proletariat and the colonized peoples had become a reality.

Peace in Indochina was almost immediately followed by war in Algeria. Immediately a change of emphasis was apparent. The rebels in Indochina had been Communists, strongly supported by both Russia and China. The Indochina war had not involved military conscription, and therefore working-class boys were not involved in the action, and the dying. Then, too, Indochina was far away, whereas France and Algeria reached across the Mediterranean in a tight and painful finger-lock. There were plenty of Arabs working in France; the French workers knew them and despised them. An old French word for "strike-breaker" is *"bedouin."* Even the poorest French families had relations who had settled in Algeria, hard-working people like themselves who were "exploiting nobody." The greatly intelligent Albert Camus said it: my family are simple people, they have exploited nobody.

The Party hesitated, equivocated, called for "peace," but not for independence. In March 1956 the Communist parliamentary deputies voted in favor of special powers that enabled the Government to do virtually as it liked in Algeria. Aimé Césaire was outraged, resigned from the Party, and wrote to Thorez, "What I desire is that Marxism and Communism should serve the Black people, not that the Black people should serve Marxism and Communism." For Fanon too this was the decisive moment of no return, the *"coupure"* with Europe. In 1957 Thorez spoke up for independence, but the Gaullist reaction in the following year involved another retreat, pious reflections about the feelings of the French masses in the face of FLN terrorism

in France, and the abandonment of the word "independence." In 1960 Thorez beat back pressure from the
non-Communist Left with the reflection that "boycotting
the war is a stupid phrase," and that "Communists must
take part in no matter which war, however reactionary."

Fanon's initial shock turned to fury—and contempt.

Every reference he made to the PCF was a verbal
Molotov cocktail. But he did not stop there; his scorn
embraced the whole French left-wing intelligentsia.
They stampeded before the accusation of treason, and
allowed themselves to be intimidated by plastic bomb
attacks and right-wing terrorism. They deplored torture, he said, because it turned young Frenchmen into
sadists and perverts, not because they had any real
concern for the Algerian victims. Georges Arnaud had
devoted a book to the execution of Djamila Bouhired;
did a single death surprise the Algerians? Simone de
Beauvoir recalls that Fanon, despite his admiration for
Sartre, "could not forget that Sartre was French, and
he blamed him for not having expiated that crime suffi-
ciently." He believed that Sartre would shake public
opinion by announcing that he would not write another
word until the war ended; "We couldn't manage to
persuade him that this wasn't so."[6]

There were two Fanons: there was the pragmatic
realist who urged the French intellectuals to ram home
to the French public the impact of the war on living
costs, taxation, and political liberty in France, and
there was the Fanon who condemned such insularity as
egocentric and sociocentric, the Fanon who wanted his
French friends to share his own subjectivity, his own
perception of the scale and horror of the war. He knew
of the heroic sacrifices made by Audin, Alleg, and his

[6] S. de Beauvoir, *Force of Circumstances* (New York, 1964),
p. 596.

own friend Francis Jeanson, whose pro-FLN resistance network was not finally crushed by the police until 1960; he knew that the left-wing press was constantly harassed and seized by the police, that students were in a state of ferment, and that radical agitation among military conscripts was increasingly paralyzing the military capability of the French Army. He knew also that it took physical as well as moral courage in an era of OAS (Secret Army Organization) terrorism to sign the famous Manifesto of the One Hundred and Twenty-one, whose signatories committed themselves in September 1960 to the support of "Frenchmen who regard it as their duty to bring help and protection in the name of the French people to oppressed Algerians." But this admirable flowering of conscience had little impact on the war. Divorced from the political parties and from the political machine, the intellectuals could not lift the burden of the struggle from the Algerian peasant in the *bled*. Fanon recognized that this was the case, yet he could not accept it. Step by step he was forced to renounce France, to renounce all hope in Europe, to recognize that the people of Algeria could depend on no one but themselves, but each step was racked by pain, incredulity, outrage. One thing was clear to him: if history had committed the Algerian peasant to violence, then he too was committed.

The step he made should not be taken for granted. *Black Skin, White Masks* is a persuasive appeal to reason and reconciliation, not an exhortation to war. Fanon was now a doctor, a healer, a professional man entrusted with a position of responsibility. Nevertheless he harbored terrorists in his home and at the hospital, provided drugs, and trained Arab nurses for the terrorist cells. In those early days of the rebellion, a high proportion of terrorist attacks were failing because the terrorists themselves were frightened or incompetent. According to Simone de Beauvoir, he taught the *Fidayines* how to control their reactions when setting a bomb and what physical and psychological attitudes to adopt under torture. All witnesses confirm that he was horrified by the violence and counterviolence, the syndrome of massacre, mutilation, and savage reprisal to which he had committed himself.

It was perhaps this repulsion which drove Fanon, by way of compensation, to regard violence not merely as a political necessity, as the only viable means of prizing apart the iron fingers of colonial rule, but also as a form of social and moral regeneration for the subjugated peoples. The flowing blood transforms the colonial dust bowl into rich and fertile national soil.

This thesis, hammered home in *The Wretched of the Earth*, is already anticipated in Fanon's essays and journalistic commentaries written in support of the Algerian rebellion. In his *Studies in a Dying Colonialism*, he portrays the armed struggle as generating a rapid liberation and modernization of Algerian social and mental structures. The use of radios was one example. Before the war, Radio-Alger not only represented the voice of the colonizing culture; its programs also offended the sensibilities and taboos of the puritanical and patrilineal Algerian family. But in 1956 the Voice of Free Algeria came on the air and within twenty days, Fanon records, the entire stock of radio sets was sold out. The more the authorities resorted to jamming, the more the presence and power of the Voice made itself felt. The tight, hermetic, and hierarchical structure of the Algerian family was now exploded; as the sons committed themselves to the resistance movement, the self-assurance and authority of the fathers was broken. The national cause provided a new focus of allegiance and authority which transcended the habit of absolute obedience to the head of the family.

And a new Algerian woman was born. Arab women who carried weapons, grenades, and messages for the FLN broke free from their traditional confinement and subjugation. For the first time women began to travel unaccompanied from Oran to Constantine or Algiers; to stay with unknown families; to give refuge in their houses to militants while their own husbands were away; to wear either European clothes, or, alternatively, the traditional protective *haïk*, as the tactics of the struggle demanded; to act on their own initiative, to develop their own personalities, to state their own opinions in the presence of male relatives, to make their own choices in marriage. "The couple became the basic cell of the commonwealth, the fertile nucleus of the nation," writes Fanon. "There is a simultaneous emergence of the citizen, the patriot, and the modern spouse."[7]

We have already seen how Fanon was inclined to raise a tendency or trend which he valued and encouraged to the level of a general reality. The Negroes of the Antilles embracing their blackness during the Second World War are here followed by the Arabs of Algeria achieving higher forms of human and sexual relations. We may be skeptical about the extent of this emancipation in practice. It is also true that Fanon's treatment of the Algerian family and the Algerian woman lacks a sociological dimension; he does not distinguish between the *fellah* in the *bled* and the urban petty bourgeois. Samuel Rohdie is correct when he comments, "In non-class terms Fanon identified the independence struggle in Algeria with a social revolu-

[7] Fanon, *Studies in a Dying Colonialism*, p. 114.

tion."[8] It is true, of course, that once again for tactical and propagandist reasons Fanon was anxious to reinforce the image of a totally united nation and to de-emphasize the internal tensions between town and country, peasant and bourgeois, which he discusses at great length in *The Wretched of the Earth*. Even taking this factor into account, the impression is strong that Fanon remained a radical liberal until 1959-1960 and that his total commitment to *socialism* and the *socialist* revolution followed later, from his observations of decolonization south of the Sahara, in black Africa. In December 1957 he described colonialism as "the conquest of a national territory and the oppression of a people; that's all." By 1960 he recognized that colonialism also involved the saturation of native society, particularly the towns, by the Western capitalist system and its values. Consequently formal independence alone had nothing to do with authentic decolonization.

A radical liberal? Obviously this characterization is incomplete. He was already a revolutionary, a Jacobin committed to violence, an intellectual sympathetic to the dialectical methodology of Marxism. Above all, he was now stating in terms of collective, national action the thesis that true freedom cannot be granted, it must be seized. This explains his argument that French attempts to modernize the Algerian family, to break the veiled, home-bound imprisonment of the Algerian women, had to be resisted. "The woman who sees without being seen frustrates the colonizer. There is no reciprocity." Fanon's attitude to the woman-question had more in common with Western liberal thought than with the traditional attitudes of Arab or African so-

[8] S. Rohdie, "Liberation and Violence in Algeria," *Studies on the Left*, May-June 1966, p. 86.

ciety, but he rejected the narrow empirical view that a good thing given has the same meaning as a good thing seized and taken. It could be objected that in some contexts Fanon argues that the colonial power "respects" and buttresses the culture of aboriginal peoples the better to encapsulate and pacify them, while in other circumstances he condemns the French employer who invites both the Algerian employee *and his wife* to a social function as a kind of rapist. The answer here (although Fanon does not provide it explicitly) is that colonial situations vary. Particularly in the British colonies of black Africa, the ruling strategy was that of indirect government, exploiting traditional forms of government, making the tribal chiefs dependent on the colonial regime for the maintenance of their power, and playing off town against country. It is the project of total political incorporation which breeds the project of total cultural assimilation. Therefore Fanon is right: the French employer's invitation to the Arab employee *and his wife* does indeed imply *Algérie française*.

Fanon illustrates the psychology of resistance to "progress" within the colonial syndrome in his discussion of medical practice. The visit of the white doctor to the Algerian *douar* was preceded by an assembling of the whole population by the police. Furthermore, many white doctors also owned vineyards or rice fields; they were true *colons*, an integral part of a coherent system whose mailed fist was represented by the police and the army. The Argentinian journalist Adolfo Gilly recalls asking a poor Bolivian miner why did he not send his son to be vaccinated in the Inter-American Health Service ambulance which was standing at the corner. The miner shot back, "Who knows what kind of filth those *gringos* are injecting, in order to turn us

Bolivians into idiots so they can better exploit us."[9]

The future of Algeria? "After the war," wrote Fanon, "a disparity between the people and what is intended to speak for them will no longer be possible." Living in Tunis, close to the Algerian Provisional Government in exile, he knew more about the tensions and faction-fights within the movement than he was prepared to discuss. He himself was close to Ben Khedda and Saad Dalheb, but Algeria had no sooner gained her independence in July 1962 than Ben Bella, supported by Colonel Boumedienne and units of the Army, swept Ben Khedda from power. A single list of candidates for the Constituent Assembly was presented to the population; Ben Bella declared that democracy was a luxury that Algeria could not afford. The Constitution of 1963 codified and legalized the monolithic state system. Despite sweeping measures of nationalization and appropriation, Algerian governments have cooperated closely with France and taken over much of the legal, bureaucratic, educational, and technical structure of the colonial regime. Then, in 1965, Boumedienne, once again with military support, swept Ben Bella from power.

Fanon proclaimed the renovating mission of armed struggle. By the end of the war, the FLN estimated Algerian deaths, including victims of starvation, at over one million out of a total population of nine million. The majority of Europeans fled, and by the end of 1962 Algerian industry was at a standstill, the harvest had not been brought in, two million were unemployed, and four million others were declared to be "without means of subsistence." The Algerian Government had no alternative but to remain dependent on

[9] A. Gilly, preface to *Studies in a Dying Colonialism*, p. 9.

French economic and technical aid and to permit France to continue atomic tests in the Sahara. Among Algerian intellectuals Fanon is widely respected, and it is said that both Ben Bella and Boumedienne have echoed his words on the revolutionary potential of the peasantry. There are today a Boulevard Frantz Fanon and a Frantz Fanon High School in Algiers. But after the victory the Algerian peasants once again dispersed, reverting to small-scale individual farming and to the eternal struggle to draw life out of the soil.

The Antilles, Africa, and the Third World

V

The islands of the Caribbean experienced a common pattern of historical penetration: conquest, colonization, the extinction of the aboriginal peoples, and the importation of West African slaves to work on the sugar and coffee plantations. In the French Empire slavery was first abolished by the Convention in 1794, reestablished under Napoleon, and then once more abolished by the Second Republic in 1848. In Britain the reformed parliament finally ended slavery in 1834. But, just as the emancipation of the Russian serfs in 1861 had not brought about any real, substantive economic emancipation, so in the Antilles Césaire's "brute beasts" continued to fertilize the "sweet cane" with their sweat. In 1958, André Malraux traveled through the poor quarters of Pointe-à-Pitre in Guadeloupe. He commented afterward that although the demands of the natives were often unreasonable, they had a right to their unreason.

Fanon felt keenly that he was not fighting for the liberation of his native soil. He told Sartre and Simone de Beauvoir, "Above all, I don't want to become a professional revolutionary."[1] In January 1958, he anxiously surveyed the political prospects for the islands of the Caribbean. His ideal was a single, federated, renovated Caribbean nation, but the obstacles were formidable: different national languages and cultures (principally British, French, and Spanish); different speeds of development in different political contexts—Jamaica, Barbados and Trinidad were on the threshold of federation and independence. The black leaders in the British islands, such as Norman Manley in Jamaica and Eric Williams in Trinidad, were closer to social democracy than to Marxism. Cheddi Jagan's Marxist movement in British Guiana offered a more hopeful prospect, but black and white politicians alike had combined to put him in quarantine. Castro and Guevara were still a year short of Havana; Fanon does not mention them. As for the French islands, the planters remained powerful, wages were low, social legislation was retarded, and elections were partly rigged. The six deputies representing the Antilles were swallowed up and lost in the Paris Chamber of Deputies. As Césaire has said, the Antilles had become full departments of France while remaining plunged in a terrible poverty.

In this same year, 1958, the Algerian war brought about the collapse of the Fourth Republic and the accession to power of de Gaulle. Determined to forestall the proliferation of Algerian-type situations throughout the French overseas territories, de Gaulle made a bold

[1] S. de Beauvoir, *Force of Circumstances* (New York, 1964), p. 595.

lunge intended to castrate the Negro revolution. He staged a referendum offering the colonies a choice of immediate independence, total integration with France, or two forms of association within a new, renovated French Community.

The French Antilles said "yes" to total integration.

Malraux, former left-wing novelist and hero of the Spanish Civil War and now a Minister of the Fifth Republic, was dispatched by de Gaulle to secure the umbilical cord which tied the Antilles and Guiana to France. This was the Malraux whose concepts of Western man and Western civilization Fanon sarcastically derided. Malraux traveled from village to village, receiving flowers and laying them at the foot of the bust of the Republic or, when she was not available, on the ubiquitous plaques commemorating Schœlcher, the enemy of slavery. At Fort-de-France, the mayor of the town, none other than Aimé Césaire, received Malraux with the words, "I salute in your person the great French nation to which we are passionately attached."[2] So much for Negritude, so much for putting "Marxism and Communism at the service of the Black people." Malraux then reminded his enraptured audience of those Martinicans who had fallen for France in two world wars—Fanon had once referred ironically to "all those niggers, all those wogs who fought to defend the liberty of France or for British civilization. . . ." Then the crowd took up the *Marseillaise*. And here Malraux, with his unique, rhapsodical bastardization of left- and right-wing metaphors, mocks what Fanon stood for and what Césaire, the biographer of the black Jacobin Toussaint L'Ouverture, had once stood for. "It was," says Malraux, "the cry of black liberty, that of Tous-

[2] A. Malraux, *Anti-Memoirs* (New York, 1968), p. 166.

saint L'Ouverture's fighters and of the eternal Jacquerie
—inextricably mixed with revolutionary hope and
physical fraternity."[3]

Now the crowd began to chant, "*Vive de Gaulle,
vive Césaire, viv'-de-Gold! viv'-Cé-zer!*" Then came the
videh, a great festive dance in which the people dis-
guised themselves as devils. According to Fanon, such
rites represented the collective catharsis of an oppressed people, but Malraux had a more cosmic interpretation. It was, he wrote, the millennial festival
in which "humanity delivered itself from itself." In
Black Skin, White Masks, Fanon had described
Césaire's ability to use his mastery of the French language to produce waves of ecstasy in Fort-de-France.
Nothing had changed—except that this magistral orator
was for the time being deploying his gifts in the service
of "the great French nation" rather than of "the Congo
roaring with forests and rivers."

In an article written in the immediate aftermath of
the referendum, Fanon's reaction was one of stunned
indignation. Reluctant as he was to dismiss Césaire as
a fallen idol and traitor, he concluded with the warning
that no leader should trade on the respect and affection
which the masses have for him when the independence
of the nation is at issue. Two years later he greeted
enthusiastically news of a three-day revolt in Martinique, where, in December 1959, rebels cut the roads
and occupied Fort-de-France for more than six hours.
Castro was now master of Cuba; Fanon turned again to
the Caribbean with renewed optimism.

But the Antilles remain to this day a part of France.

In black Africa, toward which Fanon was now pro-
jecting an impassioned gaze, the outcome of the refer-

[3] *Ibid.*, p. 168.

endum was everywhere the same except in Guinea, the single colony to choose independence. Basically, the tactics of the *Loi Cadre* had proved effective. Originally legislated in 1956 and modified in 1957, the *Loi Cadre* introduced universal suffrage on a common electoral roll in all French territories and granted wide autonomy in local affairs to the African governments. Fanon denounced the *Loi Cadre*, congresses of African radicals held at Bamako and Cotonou denounced it, and the FLN denounced it, but the effect was as intended: the African politicians both enjoyed power in their own kingdoms and could rely on French aid and investment. Admittedly, some of these politicians were more thoroughly compromised than others. Fanon's *bête noir* was the leading politician of the Ivory Coast, Félix Houphouët-Boigny, a regular member of successive French ministries and a stanch proponent of the view that Algeria should remain part of France. But if Houphouët-Boigny had never figured among Fanon's heroes, Senghor had. Yet it was under Senghor's guidance that Senegal returned a ninety-seven-per-cent "yes" vote in the referendum, the poet of Negritude himself declaring, "Voting for independence means voting for selling your peanuts in the World market." In Fanon's view, authentic decolonization meant that the first shall be last, and the last shall be first. Yet Senghor was ostentatiously installing Europeans in high administrative posts in Senegal. Fanon complained bitterly, but the sellout was an ancient and venerated tradition among Senegalese politicians. The mulatto Gabriel Pellegrin, one of the leaders of anti-French insurrection in 1802, was by 1823 the royalist government's choice as mayor of St. Louis. A century later, in 1914, the black radical Blaise Diagne was elected to represent his people in the Paris Chamber of Deputies; by 1921 he was defending the French Empire against the criticisms of W. E. B. Du Bois and the Pan-African Congress; by 1930 he had been delegated by the ultraconservative Tardieu Government to defend France's record in the matter of forced labor at the International Labor Congress. (A simple-minded *littérateur* called André Gide had visited the French Congo and then returned to propound the naïve view that the brutal forced labor he had witnessed was brutal forced labor.) As for Blaise Diagne, he continued to live in style in Dakar in a large house donated by the Bank of West Africa. Senghor had his models.

In 1960, de Gaulle's renovated French Community broke down and by the end of that year all the French colonies in West Africa had gained independence. But Fanon was fast realizing that the panacea of independence did not in itself solve Africa's problems. He spoke of the "smoky" idea of African unity and of the subjectivist stagnation of many of its supporters. In September, the federation of Mali (Senegal and the former Sudan) broke up, Dahomey and Upper Volta having seceded at an earlier date. Between radical Mali (previously the Sudan) and the conservative Houphouët-Boigny there was an obvious hostility. While Ghana, Guinea, and Mali stressed political cooperation, Liberia and Nigeria favored economic cooperation; the United Arab Republic spoke of cultural cooperation. Regionalism, tribalism, and suspicion prevailed; each party or vested interest was protecting its own "turf." Arriving in Ghana in 1960 as Ambassador of the Algerian Provisional Government, Fanon witnessed at close quarters some sordid intrigues and power-play. He came to the conclusion—another crucial element in the philosophy of *The Wretched of the Earth*—that countries that had gained independence by the peaceful, political route were in the grip of a bourgeois class as aggressive and chauvinistic as the French bourgeoisie of the Great Revolution. The refusal of black Africa to take concerted military action against the white south of the continent only deepened his disillusion.

This brought him to the third and last phase of his evolution as a social philosopher. First he had assailed prejudice and mystification; then he had turned his fire against colonialism itself; now he recognized that decolonization would be authentically revolutionary only if it was also authentically socialist. At the same time the external threat was, at least in West Africa, no longer represented by direct colonial rule. The subtler penetration of neocolonialism became enemy number one. Fanon cast his eye around the world. He was not a Communist, or indeed an orthodox Marxist, but he believed that the Soviet bloc gave more help to the new nations than did the West. Khrushchev's table-thumping rudeness and Castro's appearance in uniform at the United Nations in 1960 seemed to Fanon legitimate. About China, he said very little; the great rift between China and Russia had not yet come fully into the open. As for the United States, his attitude was uniformly hostile; he knew all about the stabilizing role of the Marines in Latin America. "Castro," he wrote in 1961, "took power in Cuba, and gave it to the people."[4] As a result, the United States was busily organizing counter-revolutionary brigades. The almighty dollar was greedily feeding off the oil wells of the Middle East, the mines of Peru and the Congo, and the plantations owned by United Fruit and Firestone. Fanon hoped to visit Cuba, but death intervened.

[4] Fanon, *The Wretched of the Earth* (New York, 1965), p. 77n.

For Fanon, the bitterest lesson in the strategy of Western neocolonialism was provided by the tragic fall and murder of his friend Patrice Lumumba, Prime Minister of the Congo. The two men were exact contemporaries at birth, and still contemporaries at death.

Lumumba's radical nationalism was of comparatively recent vintage. Both men had been addressed as *"tu"* by whites, but while Fanon was finding at least intellectual respect and freedom in France, Lumumba remained an aspiring provincial, anchored to the "heart of darkness." In a book written as recently as 1956-1957, he had said, "I believe that it would be possible, in the relatively near future, to grant political rights to the Congolese elite and to the Belgians of the Congo. . . . There would be no question of granting these rights to people who were unfit to use them, to dull-witted illiterates; that would be to put dangerous weapons in the hands of children."[5] Independence, he said, would have little meaning at the present time; what was needed was progressive reform and Africanization of the administration. Thereafter Lumumba's radicalization developed rapidly, but he was more of a Jacobin than a socialist, and his statement, "I am the Congo; the Congo has made me; I am making the Congo," is closer in spirit to Nkrumah's philosophy than to Fanon's. Certainly he stood for the unity of the Congo against the separatism of Albert Kalonji in South Kasai and of Moïse Tshombe in Katanga; certainly his principal enemies were Western mining trusts and their hired mercenaries; certainly the Western governments regarded him by the autumn of 1960 as a dangerous threat to their influence in Central Africa; and certainly Lumumba had become a passionate pan-African. But if

[5] P. Lumumba, *Congo My Country*. Translated by G. Heath (New York, 1962), p. 32.

he had survived, and if he had been able to mold social policy according to his own formulas, the result would undoubtedly have been a Congo resembling Guinea or Ghana rather than the African Cuba that Fanon now demanded.

But Fanon rightly felt Lumumba's fall as a terrible blow to the African cause. In an article published in *Afrique Action* in February 1961, he dissected the reactionary interventionist roles of the Union Minière, of the regime in Rhodesia, and finally of the United Nations. Lumumba, he argued, had been wrong to call in the United Nations; the United Nations had shown itself to be an agent of anti-Communism and of neo-colonialism (a view subsequently documented by, among others, Conor Cruise O'Brien[6]). Similarly, African states such as Ghana had made a disastrous move in sending their troops to the Congo under United Nations auspices and control. They ought, he insisted, to have intervened directly in support of Lumumba. (In practice a small state such as Ghana is bound to depend on an industrialized power for military air transport.)

Fanon himself had worked tirelessly not only for unity of purpose and action within black Africa but also between the states south of the Sahara and Algeria. Beyond this pancontinentalism he was also formulating a wider unity, that of the "Third World." As an FLN journalist he paid tribute not only to nominal socialist leaders such as Nehru, Sukarno, Nasser, and Nkrumah, but also to Bourguiba of Tunisia and the King of Morocco, the very statesmen whom (implicitly) he later scythed down as betrayers of genuine decolonization. He persuaded the ALN *maquis* to train guer-

[6] In *To Katanga and Back* (New York, 1962).

rillas for the Angolan rebel leader Holden Roberto, arguing that each act of sedition, each Jacquerie in the Third World, was related to a unifying confrontation with colonialism and neocolonialism.

The French General Maurice Challe was laying mine-fields along Algeria's borders with Tunisia and Morocco in order to cut off supplies to the *wilayas* of the ALN. In 1959, Fanon's jeep hit a mine on the Algerian-Moroccan border; he suffered twelve vertebral fractures complicated by paraplegia and sphincterian troubles. He went to Rome for medical treatment. According to an account by his Guyanese friend Dr. Bertène Juminer, the car which was to take him to Rome airport was sabotaged by counterrevolutionary terrorists of the "Red Hand." The car exploded prematurely, killing two children playing in the street. While in the hospital in Rome, Fanon noticed a press item which mentioned his presence in the hospital. He moved to another room, and that night killers burst into the room he had vacated and shot up the empty bed. Fanon became "morbidly prudent" and would never enter Juminer's apartment without first investigating the environs.[7]

The following year he arrived in Accra and set about organizing supply routes to Algeria from south of the Sahara. He envisaged "great navigation canals across the desert . . . men from Mali, from Senegal, from Guinea, from the Ivory Coast, from Ghana, from Nigeria and Togoland. May they all climb the slopes of the desert and unfurl on the colonialist bastion."[8] The decision was taken to establish a base to supply *wilayas* one and five operating in the south of Algeria. Fanon set out on a long reconnaissance mission, but the French

[7] *Présence Africaine*, 40, 1962, p. 126.
[8] Fanon, *Pour la révolution africaine*, p. 206.

intelligence services were vigilant and the mission almost ended in the interrogation cells of El Biar. Arriving at Monrovia, in Liberia, he and his companions discovered that the only available flight to Conakry, in Guinea, belonged to Air France. The exceptional solicitude of the Air France staff alerted Fanon and his friends, who wisely got away by road; the plane they had almost boarded subsequently turned east to Abidjan, in the Ivory Coast, where Houphouët-Boigny's regime was working hand in glove with the French Deuxième Bureau.

In Bamako the Mali leader Modibo Keita gave every assistance. From Bamako there followed a long and hazardous journey through Gao to Bouressa and Tamanrasset, making contacts, learning about local conditions, formulating plans. By now Fanon was in the grip of a fatal illness, leukemia, and was rapidly losing weight. He traveled to the Soviet Union for treatment and was advised there to go to Washington. In the summer of 1961 he told Juminer, "I understood that I had only three or four years more. It was necessary that I hurry to *say* and *do* the maximum . . . but my Algerian brothers asked me to look after myself."[9] His nervous energy intensified, and he threw himself into the writing of *The Wretched of the Earth*, about which Sartre declared, "The Third World discovers itself and speaks to itself through this voice."

What does the "Third World" mean? In terms of international relations and diplomacy, it means "positive neutralism" and "nonalignment" between the Western and Soviet camps. In terms of historical and economic development, it means the poor, underdeveloped nations, many of them recently colonies. Unfor-

[9] *Présence Africaine*, 40, 1962, p. 127.

tunately, these two criteria do not coincide. If the one model is imposed on the other, ragged edges are visible. At one extreme of the political spectrum China, North Vietnam, and North Korea are clearly "aligned," as are South Korea, Thailand, and many Latin American states at the other. Yugoslavia figures prominently among the nonaligned states, but her economic and industrial development is hardly in the same historical stage as that of Mali or India. What is essential to Fanon's vision of the Third World is poverty, relative nonindustrialization, and a vast peasant class struggling to raise itself and to beat back neocolonialism. It is generally the case that where the Marxist-Communist ideology officially prevails, the notion of the Third World as a distinct entity with its own mission is regarded as an aberration. Here the emphasis is on the alliance and identity of interests between the working class of the socialist states and the peasant masses of the underdeveloped nations. F. Stambouli, a Tunisian admirer of Fanon, has argued that it is a misconception that Fanon "saw the Third World in its entirety as the redeemer of mankind, on account of some claimed specificity or vocation. . . ."[10] But Stambouli shows himself generally anxious to bring "Fanon" closer into line with orthodox Marxism, and his point of view is clearly contradicted by *The Wretched of the Earth* itself.

In Fanon's view, Europe owed the Third World an immense debt which had to be repaid. He regarded European affluence and opulence as literally "scandalous," derived as it was from slavery and from the piratical robbery of the fruit of the natives' soil and subsoil. Europe, he said, is literally the creation of the

[10] F. Stambouli, "Frantz Fanon," *Revue de l'Institut de Sociologie*, No. 2/3, 1967, p. 533.

Third World. The money spent on the arms race alone would have a tremendous impact on the underdeveloped economies; therefore the Cold War had to be brought to a halt. If Adenauer was paying reparations to Israel, then why should the wealthy Western nations not follow his example? Without massive assistance from Europe, the predicament of the underdeveloped countries was a hopeless one. Reluctant to appeal exclusively to Europe's withered sense of justice, he warned that if the Third World continued to stagnate, Western capitalists would have to face factory closures at home and a new wave of proletarian unrest.

Fanon's perspective here differs most sharply from that of those who argue that before colonization the countries of Africa and Asia showed no sign of developing the will, culture, organization, or technical resources to produce an industrial liftoff. It follows from this premise that although colonialism was doubtless profitable, it was not "exploitative"—indeed it and it alone developed the base for industrial liftoff. (I leave aside the erudite idiocy of those historians who contend that the European nations stumbled into their nineteenth-century empires in a protracted fit of absentmindedness.) We cannot argue the case in detail here. It is true, however, that in many parts of the world the colonial Crusoe, far from bringing the benefits of economic initiative to desert wastes, actively deformed and sometimes destroyed thriving civilizations and growing economies. It is also known that from the sixteenth to the nineteenth centuries about fifteen million slaves were shipped from Africa to the Americas, not counting those lost in the "middle passage," such as the one hundred and seventy-three sick slaves jettisoned in mid-ocean by the slave ship *Zong* in 1781. In 1788 the British West Indian sugar planters valued their holdings at seventy million pounds. It was such ports as Liverpool and Bristol, grown rich on the slave trade, that provided the initial capital surplus for the industrial revolution in Britain. The profits reaped from the colonies by latter-day capitalism are prodigious. One cannot quarrel with Fanon when he states that "deportations, massacres, forced labor, slavery, have been the principal means used by capitalism to augment its reserves of gold and diamonds, its wealth, and to establish its power." Nor did he exaggerate the grinding poverty to which vast tracts of the Third World find themselves condemned; in 1959, Mali's average annual income per capita was fifty-two dollars. It is also generally the case that the lower the per-capita income, the lower the growth rate, and the greater the dependence on fluctuations in the world market for primary crops and raw materials. But as to what constitutes "exploitation," men do not agree.

We might solve the problem by inventing a Brechtian parable: The white man comes to the wide and roaring river; he jumps on the black man's back and shouts to him, "Swim!" The black man toils and finally reaches the far bank, exhausted; his hand reaches up for recompense, but the white man is indignant. "Without me," he says, "you would never have crossed the river."

On Revolution and Violence

vi

The Wretched of the Earth was written and
published during the last year of Fanon's life,
and it is on this book that his present reputation
and influence primarily rest. Unlike his earlier
work, this culminating *chef d'œuvre* is sys-
tematically sociological. Fanon steps back from
the Algerian war, which was still in progress,
and surveys the predicament of the Third World
in general. And he does so with a vibrating,
relentless passion, a prophet writing at white
heat. But it is not an easy book to interpret.
Fanon's passion for aphorisms is often indulged
at the expense of precision. Or the clarity is
spurious. Sweeping generalizations are offered
usually without concrete evidence. The wide
canvas of the Third World is filled in with
sweeping strokes of a brush almost exclusively
dipped in African paint. About Asia, he says

nothing. The narrative drives forward in the present tense, but here his sense of historical sequence loses itself in an elliptical oscillation between past and present, present and future, future and past. Once again "is" and "ought," the actual and the ideal, are subsumed in a single categorical affirmation. Socialist revolutions for which there is neither model nor precedent walk Fanon's pages with as much assurance as instances of degeneration whose actual sources are easy to guess. The Algerian revolution is implicitly treated as a model for all of Africa; a set of unitary ideals and categories is imposed on a continent outstanding for its size and diversity. And yet *The Wretched of the Earth* is one of the great political documents of our time.

First his laser beam pierces the black and brown bourgeoisie of the colonial towns. The Western bourgeoisie is both productive and parasitical; the colonial bourgeoisie is simply parasitical. Lacking all skill as entrepreneurs, they were content to act as agents for Western companies. They readily exploited the native proletariat and peasantry, they were completely divorced from and contemptuous of the rural population, they wallowed in luxury goods and invested their money abroad. Far from taking any creative role in the production of national wealth, they gravitated toward intermediary activities as retailers, professional men, lawyers, civil servants, army officers, politicians.

About this Fanon was perfectly correct. Although his strictures were largely based on personal observation of society in Ghana and the Ivory Coast, the generalization held good. A study of a Nigerian sample elite conducted in 1958 showed that seventy-five per cent were engaged in the professions, politics, and administration. In 1955, only 0.1 per cent of the Algerian

Arab (or Muslim) population was classified as industrialist. No doubt the colonial system was to blame, but that was not the point. Or rather it was, for the native bourgeoisie was both created by colonialism and saturated by its worst paternalistic and racist poisons.

In the phase of the struggle against colonialism, Fanon continued, the native bourgeoisie formed the backbone of the Nationalist parties. Originally progressive and patriotic, these parties rapidly degenerated into agencies for the transfer of power and privilege from a few white hands to a few black ones. Sometimes violent in their language, Nationalist parties were invariably cautious, reformist, and nonviolent in their performance. (Fanon did not admire Gandhi.) They never broke off the dialogue with colonialism. They might cash in on the results of armed rebellion, but they never organized it. Not a single well-known Nationalist in Kenya had claimed membership of the Mau Mau or openly defended it. Divorced from and hostile toward the rural populations, the Nationalist parties drove the political opposition into retrograde, tribalist forms. At all costs, the national liberation movement had to be wrested from the grasp of the bourgeoisie.

In that case, what combination of social forces would insure the integrity of the revolution?

According to the classic scheme of Marx and Engels, in the industrially mature, capitalist societies, it is the urban proletariat, the working class, which constitutes the revolutionary social force. It is this universal class which will establish its own dictatorship as a preliminary to communism itself. Marx disavowed a unilinear theory of history and did not insist that all areas of the world had to pass through the capitalist experience. He suggested, tentatively it is true, that the Russian peasantry might transport their society direct from the feudal to the socialist stage. But with Lenin the emphasis reverts to the proletariat as the essential vanguard of a revolutionary alliance of the workers and the poorest classes of peasantry. And if such an alliance was necessary in Russia, it was even more indispensable in Asia and Africa, where the proletariat constituted only a tiny fraction of the population. Neither Trotskyists, Stalinists, nor Maoists have ever departed *in theory* from this concept of the proletarian vanguard; they have never admitted the possibility of a viable peasant revolution. Nor have they abandoned *in theory* the thesis of a fundamental sympathy and identity of interests between the Western proletariat and the colonial peoples. Lenin, it is true, drew attention to a "proletarian aristocracy" grown relatively fat on colonial spoils, but he intended only to describe a minority phenomenon and one which would be obliterated in the general crisis of capitalist imperialism.

Therefore Fanon was not a Marxist in any traditional sense.

He regarded the Western proletariat as neither revolutionary nor sympathetic to the colonial peoples. The Western workers were, in his opinion, the beneficiaries and accomplices of latter-day colonialism. Here the Algerian war was the decisive experience for Fanon. He referred to the often bloodthirsty enthusiasm of French workers and peasants fighting the FLN. He noted the heroes' welcome given by the popular masses of Paris to Massu's paratroopers on July 14, 1957. Had not the French Communist Party justified its equivocations in terms of working-class sentiment? Fanon was by no means alone in reaching these conclusions. Senghor described the solidarity between the Western workers and the colonial people as a romatic illusion.

Sartre, too, had traveled this route. We see that in the early 1950s he, like Fanon, was subscribing to the Marxian equation of the proletariat with the universal class. In 1948 he did suggest that the white worker, *in spite of himself*, profited *a little* from the colonies. By 1960 both the "in spite of himself" and the "a little" had vanished from Sartre's scathing analysis of European working-class ideology.

Fanon's argument has been criticized by Marxists of varying tendencies. Michel Pablo, a Trotskyist critic, blamed the leadership of the reformist Socialist and revisionist Communist parties for the paralysis of the European workers. Therefore Fanon had mistaken a temporary political deformation for a permanent sociological one.[1] On the other hand, spokesmen for the Soviet-bloc states insist that it is to the proletariat of the socialist states that the colonial masses should turn so long as the Western workers are fettered by the power of capitalism and bourgeois propaganda.

Fanon now goes a stage further: he dismisses the revolutionary nature and potential of the native proletariat in the colonies. Like the colonial bourgeoisie, the colonial working class enjoyed a privileged and well-remunerated position under foreign rule; it too was generally loyal to the electoralist Nationalist parties. (It is therefore a simplification to interpret Fanon as metaphorically describing the whole colonized populations—minus the rich—as the "proletariat" of the modern world politico-economic system, and the whole population of the metropolitan powers as the "bourgeoisie.") For this thesis Fanon was even more sharply attacked, notably by the Vietnamese Communist Nguyen Nghe: "The peasant by himself can never

[1] M. Pablo, "Les damnés de la terre," *Quatrième Internationale*, 15, 1962, p. 62.

develop a revolutionary consciousness; it is the militant who comes from the towns who must patiently search out the most gifted elements of the poor peasantry, and educate them. . . ."[2] According to Nghe, Fanon's critical analysis of the colonial proletariat foundered on his failure to distinguish between genuinely proletarian elements such as dockers and miners, and petty-bourgeois groups such as taxi-drivers and clerks. Fanon had been misled by the fact that the decisive battles in China, Vietnam, Cuba, and Algeria had taken place in the countryside, with peasants comprising the bulk of the guerrilla forces. But the leadership of urban elements —intellectuals and workers—was indispensable. "A permanent peasant revolution can only be a Jacquerie without a future." This general approach was endorsed by the Soviet scholar I. I. Potekhin: "The African working class has to fulfill a specific historical mission—to take the initiative in establishing a socialist system of production and to lead the peasantry in this task."[3]

Which brings us to the core of Fanon's theory—that the authentic revolutionary class in the Third World, and indeed in the world today, was the poor peasantry, the victims of absolute impoverishment but men and women with a sense of community, "a coherent people who go on living, as it were, statically, but who keep their moral values and their devotion to the nation intact."[4] Generous in spirit, ready to give protection to the urban militant pursued by the security forces, prepared to reclaim their soil and their dignity by vio-

[2] N. Nghe, "Frantz Fanon," *La Pensée*, February 1963, p. 29.
[3] See W. Friedland and C. Rosberg (eds.), *African Socialism* (Stanford, Calif., 1964), p. 104.
[4] Fanon, *The Wretched of the Earth* (New York, 1965), p. 101.

lence, these men and women were the veritable "wretched of the earth," *les damnés de la terre*. (The phrase is taken from the first line of the *Internationale*, and its use was perhaps suggested to Fanon by two poems of the Haitian Communist Jacques Roumain, whom he much admired. The general theory of peasant revolution, of the sickle not the hammer, is anticipated in Abdoulaye Ly's book *Les masses africaines et l'actuelle condition humaine* [1956].)

Fanon delineates the progress of the revolution along the following lines. The rebellion begins, takes root, and structures itself militarily in the countryside, then filters into the towns through the uprooted peasants, the *Lumpenproletariat* living in the shanty towns, those who have not yet succeeded in finding "a bone to gnaw in the colonial system." In this class the rebellion finds its urban spearhead. "They are like a horde of rats; you may kick them and throw stones at them, but despite your efforts they'll go on gnawing at the roots of the tree."[5] These "classless idlers," pimps, prostitutes, and petty criminals (strongly denounced by Marx in *The 18th Brumaire of Louis Bonaparte*) are, according to Fanon, "rehabilitated in their own eyes and those of history."

Yet Fanon provides no examples, and it is difficult to find the actual instances on which such a theory could safely rest, although, during the Algerian war, the *Lumpenproletariat* of the Casbah, the slum quarter of Algiers, did take up the FLN's battle in the town. Zolberg has cited these passages as proof of Fanon's bent for metaphysics, and speaks of his "hallucinatory imagery which links him with Rimbaud and Jean

5 *Ibid.*, p. 103.

Genet." The city goes up in flames and the damned are purified in its fire; they are beautiful and holy.[6] Hannah Arendt accuses Fanon of "rhetorical excesses," a judgment which it is difficult to contest. While it is perfectly possible that pimps and prostitutes and swindlers may show idealism and self-sacrifice in the heat of the struggle, what is absolutely improbable is that the struggle will transform them into productive citizens of the future socialist nation. Nor would it be useful to describe the former pimps and prostitutes of Havana as Fidel's most ardent admirers. Fanon fails to distinguish between the hard-core, corrupted *Lumpenproletariat*, and the migrant peasants who move to and fro between town and village, and who are more capable of the revolutionary activity he describes and desires. Kenya and Portuguese Guinea are cases in point.

In one respect Nghe is right: Fanon failed to distinguish between the attitudes of the different urban classes. The African worker's wage, although superior to the peasant's income, produces a higher standard of living only if he throws off his dependents. The worker has no choice except to join the Nationalist Party, but his project in doing so is normally more radical than that of the businessman, civil servant, or taxi-driver. Even so, his revolutionary potential is minimal. As for Nghe's contention that "urban militants, intellectuals and workers" bring indispensable leadership to the rural guerrillas, in Mao's army, Giap's army, Castro's guerrilla units, and the ALN in Algeria, middle-class intellectuals heavily outweighed urban workers in influence. There is also the quantitative aspect to consider. In Tanganyika before independence, only 2.5 per cent of the population lived in towns, and only 4.5 per

[6] A. Zolberg, "Frantz Fanon," *Encounter*, November 1966, p. 66.

cent of the Gold Coast population were wage-earners (industrial and agricultural). A survey taken in Algeria, an economically advanced country by African standards, revealed that in 1954 73.2 per cent of the Arabs were engaged in agriculture, and that only 4.6 per cent were skilled workers.[7] The urban populations of Africa were frequently ethnically divided and therefore politically divided, the unions were weak, and in Fanon's time part-time migrant labor predominated over full-time regular labor. In the Congo, the least radical province was in 1960 the most industrialized, Katanga; the most rebellious areas were the poorest ones, where wage-earners were regarded as envied beneficiaries of material progress. One searches Guevara's writings in vain for any news of the indispensability of urban workers to successful guerrilla warfare. The conclusion seems inescapable that, whether or not Fanon was correct in identifying the African peasantry as a revolutionary class, contemporary Africa offers no other.

Fanon *defines* social classes according to Marxist criteria (relationship to the means of production, and *which* means of production). But he assesses their political behavior in terms of (a) their level of livelihood, (b) their size, and (c) the extent of their integration in the colonial system. His stress on (a) and (b) is methodologically a departure from Marxism. In this connection the influence of Sartre's *Critique of Dialectical Reason* (1960) is obvious, particularly the emphasis on "need" and "scarcity" as the historically and economically primary causes of social violence. The ensuing dialectic of praxis and the practice-inert precedes the formation of classes and the division of labor,

[7] F. M. Gottheil, "Fanon and the Economics of Colonialism," *Review of Economics and Business*, Autumn 1967, p. 74.

persists as an important factor in class society, and may continue to function even under socialism. It follows that the impoverishment of the colonized peasantry is likely to generate a radical praxis, while the relative affluence of the working class fosters reformist opportunism.

Fanon's commitment to socialism pervades the pages of *The Wretched of the Earth*. He had noted with enthusiasm the stand taken by the Cotonou congress of African radicals (1958) in favor of socialism and collectivization. He was convinced that the only means of breaking the power of the trusts, of transforming a nominal independence into a real one, of beating back neocolonialism, was to nationalize both the productive and the trading sectors. But nationalization in itself was not sufficient; there must be radical decentralization and mass democratic participation in cooperative enterprises. At the national level, integral planning, austerity, and education were the keys to progress.

Fanon was insistent, for the sociological reasons already given, that the national liberation movement and the socialist revolution must be welded together in a single, simultaneous, renovating upheaval. "In underdeveloped countries, the bourgeoisie should not be allowed to find the conditions necessary for its existence and growth." Samuel Rohdie has argued that in this respect Fanon is guilty of a confusion which the old Comintern leaders such as Lenin and M. N. Roy avoided. They based their strategy on a two-phase campaign: first, the bourgeois-nationalist revolution, during which the working-class parties offered a tactical alliance to the national bourgeoisie, and then, after independence had been achieved and a new polarization of class antagonisms built up within the nation, the socialist revolution. Rohdie is right to make the distinction, but the lessons of twentieth-century history support on balance Fanon's perspective. Even though the Russian revolution took place in two phases (March and November 1917), the Bolsheviks found it necessary to strike before the bourgeoisie could consolidate their power, and in this they were assisted by the continuation of Russia's desperate war against Germany. The successful Communist revolutions in China and Indochina were simultaneously national wars of liberation and socialist revolutions; Chiang Kai-shek was never permitted to establish a bourgeois state throughout China. The only authentically indigenous socialist revolution to have succeeded in Europe, that in Yugoslavia, was totally integrated in the struggle for national independence. One searches in vain for an example of the two-stage strategy operating effectively. The periodic upheavals in the Arab countries belong to a different mechanism altogether. Wherever the national bourgeoisie has established its power in Africa or Asia, it has retained that power.

Therefore Fanon laid great stress on the importance of correct ideological leadership in the course of the struggle against colonialism. "For my part, the more I penetrate the cultures [of Africa] and the political circles, the more certain I become that the great danger which threatens Africa is the absence of ideology. The task of bringing the people to maturity will be made easier by the thoroughness of the organization and by the high intellectual level of its leaders."[8] The trouble here is that he did not tackle the problems of constructing a socialist economy and society in any detail.

Most "socialist" leaders in Africa have insisted that African society is either fundamentally classless or

---

[8] Fanon, *The Wretched of the Earth*, p. 117.

without significant class antagonisms. This point of view has been canvassed by Senghor, Touré, Nkrumah, Madeira Keita, and Nyerere. In Senegal and Tanzania, socialism appears to be officially defined as a certain attitude of mind; Senghor speaks of an African symbiosis of moral and religious values with the "revolutionary tradition." In Ghana and Guinea, socialism has been approached in a more operationally definable institutional way. But here again there is vagueness; Touré's ideal African socialist state is a *"communau-cratie,"* a Rousseau-esque system representing the will of the whole people rather than of any single class. Nkrumah permitted some Marxist teaching at the Ideological Training Centre at Winneba, while the Accra newspaper, *The Spark*, derived from a Marxist perspective the belief in the existence of an essentially classless precolonial African society. But in January 1962 Nkrumah declared flatly that there was no class struggle in African "native" society. His treatise *Consciencism* (1964) joined in the view that native "communalism" was the natural ancestor of modern socialism, which would evolve organically by a process of perpetual reform. Meanwhile, in the east, Tom Mboya of Kenya remarked, "When I talk of 'African Socialism' I refer to those proved codes of conduct in the African societies which have, over the ages, conferred dignity on our people. . . ."

As regards practical policy, early nationalization measures in Guinea were halted in 1962, when a new code was legislated guaranteeing foreign investors against expropriation. A similar law followed in Ghana in April 1963, after Nkrumah had told a dinner of businessmen, "We on our part welcome every honest investor who wants to work for his equitable profits, but we shall not tolerate anyone who seeks to direct what political course we should follow." But this, of course, is nonsense; the very guarantee against expropriation indicates a surrender of political sovereignty.

Since Fanon did not comment directly on the "classless, communalist" theory of African socialism, we are forced to rely on inference rather than reference. He appears to attribute the formation of classes in Africa mainly to colonialism itself. As a result there is a *direct* class struggle between the peasantry and the urban bourgeoisie, and an *indirect* conflict of interests between the peasantry and the proletariat. At the same time, the conflict between the urban Nationalist parties and the tribal chiefs is more political than economic (but this was also true of the conflict between the eighteenth-century French bourgeoisie and the landed aristocracy). Since the native bourgeoisie and proletariat have relatively weak roots in the productive structure, a determined and united revolutionary peasantry ought to be able to dispose of them, and of the tribal chiefs, without a too-protracted class conflict. Just as Fanon wanted Algerian women to remove their own veils rather than have them lifted by the French, so he wanted the peasantry of Africa to settle accounts with their own chiefs rather than allow the Nationalist parties to do it—as happened, for example, in Ghana.

But this is to talk—as Fanon himself does—in general Western sociological categories. The actual structures of African society, and the actual structures of African precolonial political institutions, are extremely varied, and there can be no doubt that these variations and divisions have played an important role in complicating African political development in the 1960s. An African tribe or group may be individualistic as regards production but cooperative in the sphere of consumption; it may practice mutual aid but within tight confines. In some areas large landowners were nonexistent, whereas in Ethiopia, Buganda, northern Nigeria, and North Cameroon they were prevalent. The Hausa states or areas are strongly stratified. This is also true of the Ngwato, Bemba, Banyankole, and Kede tribes, where political organization was hierarchical before and during colonization. On the other hand, the Logoli, Tallensi, and Nuer tribes lacked sharp class divisions and centralized government. Nor is colonialist practice and the colonialist mentality absent from African society. Within the areas controlled by the Kede tribe, for example, the lowest stratum consisted of "original inhabitants" whom Kede tradition depicted as primitive, somewhat contemptible, and without a viable culture. Fanon does not discuss these differentiations. Sometimes he alludes to them or their effects indirectly, as when he complains about outbreaks of "racism" in the new, independent states, but his view of "Africa" and its social formations remains unilluminatingly schematic. He had a single vision for the continent and a single solution. The solution is compounded of correct ideology, integrity on the part of Westernized African intellectuals, and the fierce will to avoid compromise.

These outbreaks of "racism" would be better described as outbreaks of "tribalism"—a problem that raises the whole question of the new African "nation." Describing Negroism or Arabism as obsolete, Fanon insisted that the nation had to be the unit of social and moral renovation. "The first necessity is the re-establishment of the nation in order to give life to national culture in the strictly biological sense of the phrase."[9] He writes of the peasants' devotion to the nation and

9 *Ibid.*, p. 197.

the native bourgeoisie's failure to concert a policy which is genuinely national. Against the particularisms of tribalism and the vague, cosmic cults of Negroism and Arabism, he identifies the nation as the organic unit of loyalty and progress.

Now even in Europe states and nations are not invariably identical. Germany today comprises one nation and two states; Czechoslovakia comprises two nations and one state. The states of modern Africa are predominantly the creations of European imperialism, and the lines dividing them were generally dictated less by tribal or ethnic considerations than by European rivalries and administrative convenience. The Cameroons, for example, are divided by language (British and French) and also by religion. Nigeria was created with a Muslim-Hausa North, a predominantly Yoruba West, and an Ibo-majority East. The present war in Biafra speaks for itself. The "nation" that Lumumba wanted to hold together in the Congo was a European creation. Ghana and Mali are symbolic names referring to medieval empires; modern Ghana is not a natural national entity. Whereas the boundary of Ghana and Togoland runs north-south, the cultural zones run east-west, so that the large Ewe tribe is spread across the southern regions of both states. Even in a small land area such as Ghana there is a multiplicity of languages, and sometimes Africans born fifty miles apart make effective communication only in English.

It is curious that Fanon, who wanted to snap the bonds of European culture, should have transformed arbitrary European structures into the natural units of African progress. Since these separate states exist, and dreams of pan-African federation have receded, it may be a case of *faute de mieux*, but it is difficult to see local sense in his concept of the "re-establishment of the nation . . . in the strictly biological sense of the phrase."

The Fanonian process of decolonization is not only national in form but violent in content. Colonialism is violence, political, military, cultural, and psychic; only a counterviolence operating in the same spheres can eradicate it. There exists a complicated discussion of what Marx said about violence and how he related it to the overthrow of different state systems, and of whether Lenin's interpretation of Marx in this respect was more accurate than, for example, Karl Kautsky's. Marx said that force is the midwife of history, but he qualified this generalization in the 1860s and 1870s with respect to the bourgeois-democratic state systems then prevailing in Britain, Holland, and the United States. In such conditions, he said, the proletariat might achieve power by nonviolent means. In the 1890s Engels included France and Germany in this perspective. In his own discussion of collective violence, Fanon made no reference to the various arguments within the Marxist movement. Rather, it was his own direct observations of Algeria and Africa which transformed his early existential view of violence as a form of radical, humanistic self-assertion by the individual (nonviolent violence, in fact), into a systematic theory of the necessity of collective, revolutionary violence in the Third World. One can speculate about more immediate intellectual influences on Fanon. Merleau-Ponty had argued in his *Humanisme et Terreur* (1947) that violence is built into the historical dialectic and that this violence had to embrace all those who were *objectively* enemies of the revolution. Since violence was an integral element of presocialist society, the only question, according to Merleau-Ponty, was which form of social violence worked toward the suppression of all violence.

Sartre developed this line of reasoning in his play *The Devil and the Good Lord* (1951), in his long articles *The Communists and the Peace* (1953), in his controversy with Camus (1952), and in his later *Critique of Dialectical Reason*. And no writer exercised a greater influence on Fanon than Sartre.

Fanon believed that in a revolutionary confrontation the colonizing forces were doomed. He dismissed as "childish" Engels' argument in *Anti-Dühring* that the triumph of violence depends on the production of arms and therefore on economic strength in general. The success of the armed revolution, says Fanon, rests on three factors: (a) the ardor of the colonized peoples, (b) the fact that colonies are now markets and protracted warfare is therefore not in the interests of the trusts, and (c) the fact that the Cold War inflames Western fears that the Communists will infiltrate colonial risings. No colonial power was capable of maintaining indefinitely the large occupation forces required to hold a nation down. The word "indefinitely" seals the argument, but it is worth mentioning that by 1964 the Angolan guerrillas were confronted by a quarter of a million Portuguese *colons* and fifty thousand troops. Today, nearly a decade after the outbreak of the rebellion, the Portuguese grip looks formidable. In Kenya, the armed insurrection had been suppressed some years before independence was granted. Much depends on the political structure of the metropolitan power and its domestic and global calculations. A large settler community, such as the one in Rhodesia, breaks away from the "weak" mother country and organizes its own ruthless system of repression. South Africa is historically the classic case.

Fanon does not figure among the major theoreticians of guerrilla warfare. He confined himself to insisting that spontaneous insurrection must rapidly be replaced by systematic organization and strategy, and that scattered guerrilla units must be ultimately welded into a national army guided by a central strategy. In Fanon's lifetime guerrilla warfare had not been successfully developed south of the Sahara. The Mau Mau rising in Kenya and the rural warfare in the Congo did not progress far beyond the level of anticolonialist tribal Jacqueries. The Congolese peasants, often armed only with *pou-pou*, flung themselves into battle drugged, quite frequently, on hemp. Fanon's notes on his 1960 journey from Mali up to the Sahara are brief but precise. He envisaged that each commando unit would start out with twenty or twenty-five members, swelling later to a hundred or a hundred and fifty as local recruits were incorporated. The initial task would not be to strike at the enemy but to awaken the populations, to prize loose the myth of the enemy's strength, and to demonstrate the power of the ALN. Each commando unit would recruit three or four members from each tribe on its journey, leaving behind some of its original members. This would insure ethnic and organizational continuity along the supply routes, while providing the commando units with guides who knew the local terrain, both geographical and political.

In Mao's teachings, it is the Communist Party which guides the guerrilla campaigns, whereas according to Fanon, Guevara, and Régis Debray, the revolutionary party grows out of the guerrilla campaigns. Guevara and Debray regard the old-style Communist parties of Latin America as compromised or irrelevant; in black Africa they scarcely existed. Fanon views the African urban-based Nationalist parties in precisely the same pejorative perspective. But he differs from Guevara and Debray—particularly Debray—who portray the guerrilla nucleus as initially independent of the peasant population, and only gradually incorporating it in the struggle by means of propaganda and successful military action—the most effective type of propaganda. Fanon agrees that intellectual guidance is essential to the peasantry, but he is the more "Marxist" in attributing to the social class itself the original revolutionary impulse. Guevara and Debray, as explicit strategists, attach greater weight to nuclear military and political leadership and to revolutionary discipline; Fanon's vision is more romantic and chiliastic—a great forest fire roars through the colony. The present situation in Portuguese Guinea, where Cabral holds both the political and military leadership of the liberation movement, conforms more closely to the Guevara-Debray model.

The words "romantic" and "chiliastic" bring us to one of the most fiercely debated aspects of Fanon's later philosophy—his belief in the existential necessity of collective violence for the colonized peoples. In *Black Skin, White Masks* he had written, "There is a zone of nonbeing, an extraordinarily sterile and arid region, an utterly naked declivity, where an authentic upheaval can be born. In most cases, the black man lacks the advantage of being able to accomplish this descent into a real hell." In his own case, the inhibiting factor was clearly stated. "I do not trust fervor. Every time it has burst out somewhere, it has brought fire, famine, misery. . . . And contempt for man."[10] Now he saw fire, famine, and misery in a new light. "Violence alone, violence committed by the people, violence organized and educated by its leaders, makes it possible for the masses to understand social truths and gives the

[10] Fanon, *Black Skin, White Masks* (New York, 1967), pp. 10 and 11.

key to them."[11] Violence on a national scale liquidates tribalism and regionalism and binds the community together, committing each individual in his own eyes and the eyes of others. It would be tempting, but wrong, to substitute the word "struggle" for "violence"; under Gandhi's leadership the Indian people had engaged in collective struggle, but Fanon rejected the tactics of nonviolence as an inauthentic form of decolonization. In his preface to *The Wretched of the Earth*, Sartre repeated Fanon's proposition. "The native cures himself of colonial neurosis by thrusting out the settler through force of arms. When his rage boils over, he rediscovers his lost innocence and he comes to know himself in that he creates himself. . . . To shoot down a European is to kill two birds with one stone, to destroy an oppressor and the man he oppresses at the same time."[12] Is this to distort Fanon, to put an essentially social dialectic on the level of an existential and individual one? Apparently not, for Fanon himself is categorical on the point: "At the level of individuals, violence is a cleansing force. It frees the native from his inferiority complex and from his despair and inaction."[13] Evidently all forms of exploitation are *not* identical; evidently the colonized native is more radically crushed and dehumanized than the European worker. His subjugation is not only economic and social; it is generic.

Sartre himself had been independently pursuing a parallel path. Eight years earlier he had written, "*Les classes ne sont pas, on les fait*" (roughly, "Classes don't exist, they are made"). And he added that for the pro-

[11] Fanon, *The Wretched of the Earth*, p. 118.
[12] J.-P. Sartre, Preface to *The Wretched of the Earth*, pp. 18–19.
[13] Fanon, *The Wretched of the Earth*, p. 74.

letarian, the violent political strike was a manner of becoming a man. We can describe this doctrine as existential therapy within the context of Marxist class categories. Fanon sees the colonial world as not only oppressive but static, locked, petrified: it had to be burst asunder. Marx and Engels and Lenin had not regarded social violence in this light. The worker's violence was pragmatic, not existential; it was a structural, not a psychic, necessity. Césaire has said of Fanon that "without paradox, his violence was that of a non-violent man, I mean it was the violence of justice, purity, of intransigence."[14] The "without paradox" is not so easy to swallow. The violent doctrines of the neofascist Italian Futurists could be justified by the same formula. Fanon wrote to Juminer that "action is incoherence and agitation if it does not restructure the consciousness of the individual."[15] But this is simply a tautology.

Fanon's views on violence have been widely compared to those of Georges Sorel's *Reflections on Violence* (1908). Sorel had written, "It is to violence that socialism owes its high moral values through which it brings salvation to the modern world."[16] Hannah Arendt, having drawn attention to Sorel's debt to Henri Bergson's concept of *élan vital*, remarks that Fanon "was greatly influenced by Sorel's equation of violence, life and creativity. . . ."[17] According to Zolberg, Fanon believed that the black masses needed a "myth," just as Sorel believed that the European proletariat needed a myth. But Fanon's debt to Sorel is highly

[14] *Présence Africaine*, 40, 1962, p. 119.
[15] *Ibid.*, p. 126.
[16] G. Sorel, *Réflexions sur la violence* (Paris, 1950), p. 389.
[17] H. Arendt, "Reflections on Violence," *New York Review of Books*, February 27, 1969, p. 29.

problematical. He never mentions him. Sorel, who later flirted with fascism, had become a bad name on the Left. In his preface, Sartre writes, "If you set aside Sorel's fascist utterances, you will find that Fanon is the first since Engels to bring the processes of history into the clear light of day."[18] This statement is in itself not convincing. It simply supports the view that Fanon would not have acknowledged any debt to Sorel. In fact, Sartre's own assertion about the proletarian and the political strike, quoted above, is highly Sorelian.

We can leave the question of derivations for that of essences. Is Fanon's doctrine of violence substantially the same as Sorel's? If it is, we have to remember that Sorel's theory of violence carried him in the space of a few years from admiration of Lenin to admiration of Mussolini. The notion of "myth" is crucial for Sorel, who wrote, "One can judge myths as means of acting on the present." But this concept of "myth" is never accepted by Fanon. Sorel was a pessimist and an antirationalist; he distrusted theories of progress and of the inevitable success of proletarian revolution. Therefore in Sorel *the proletariat violently asserts itself in an oppressive society without necessarily overthrowing that society*. Violence here is indeed a form of collective *élan vital*. The foundations of Fanon's theory are quite different; for him the peasant revolution is not a myth but a reality; it is not only "a means of acting on the present" but also a means of overthrowing the present. It is within the context of effective social action that violence is renovating.

However, objections to Fanonian violence are not

necessarily bourgeois objections. Nguyen Nghe has pointed out, *à propos* Fanon, that wars of liberation do not last for ever and that the violent experiences which men undergo in their course may create as many problems as they resolve. He observes that after nine years in the *maquis*, many Vietnamese resistance fighters did not know what to do with themselves and returned to their opium. Social construction is liable to seem slow and prosaic compared to social destruction, as Guevara discovered.

No man, no peasant, is purely a social being, a member of a particular class or race. When he kills a class enemy or an oppressor, he also kills *another man*. All killing is by definition dehumanizing. The peasant wins his war, but he loses a particular battle. The curious thing is that we have only to turn to Fanon himself to find evidence of this. His psychiatric case histories concern not only the victims but also the perpetrators of violence. An African militant had planted a bomb in a cafe, killing ten. Every year, at about the same time, he suffered from acute anxiety, insomnia, and suicidal obsessions. An Algerian whose own mother had been wantonly murdered himself wantonly killed a white woman who was on her knees begging for mercy. As a result, he suffered what Fanon calls an anxiety psychosis of the depersonalization type. Fanon's own close involvement with and understanding of such cases makes his theory of renovating violence more difficult to understand. It is said that while he was studying medicine in Lyons his hand had shaken uncontrollably when he performed autopsies.

One appreciates that he was greatly incensed by what he observed in independent black Africa, particularly in Ghana. He states that where decolonization has been evolutionary and relatively nonviolent, the emergent nation is controlled by "know-all, smart, wily intellectuals," who resort to legal robbery, import-export combines, stock-exchange jobbery, and so forth, to cheat their own people. However true this may be, Fanon could usefully have distinguished between settler and nonsettler colonialism, between those colonies where a sizeable class of whites owned and farmed the land (Algeria, Kenya, Rhodesia) and those where they did not (most of West Africa). In the latter areas a dialogue between the native bourgeoisie and the metropolitan country was always possible, whereas in Algeria or Kenya the *colons* intervened. Fanon did not want the white man to *grant* the black man anything, but it is difficult to seize independence by force once it has been promised for a specific date in the near future. He himself noted that the development of anticolonial violence was proportionate to the repression exercised by the regime. But if, as he says, the peasant's first objective is to seize the settler's farm, his land, what can be expected where there are no settlers and no white farms? How then can nonauthentic decolonization and bourgeois rule be prevented?

Fanon wanted a Caesarean birth. He wanted Africa to tear itself free from Europe and Europe's values. "When I search for Man in the technique and the style of Europe, I see only a succession of negations of man, an avalanche of murders." Europe, he said, "undertook the leadership of the world with ardor, cynicism and violence. . . . Europe has declined all humility and modesty; but she has also set her face against all solicitude and all tenderness. . . . So, comrades, let us not pay tribute to Europe by creating states, institutions and societies which draw their inspiration from her . . . we must turn over a new leaf, we must work out new

concepts, and try to set afoot a new man."[19] Fanon had
turned his back on Europe. Or had he? In one of his
prefaces, *Orphée Noir* (1948), Sartre had claimed that
Negro poetry was written by Negroes for Negroes. Now
he took up this theme again, telling his European
readers: Fanon often speaks of you, but never to you;
you are merely zombies listening in to a private conversation. In both cases an apparent statement of fact
is really a misleading metaphor; in both cases it is
Sartre, a white Frenchman, who has been invited to
write a preface in French to a book initially published
in Paris. It was Fanon who sent the manuscript of *The
Wretched of the Earth* to Sartre, hoping he would write
the preface; just as, at an earlier date, Cheik Anta
Diop had upheld his celebrated thesis on African cultural history before an examining board of French pro-
fessors in the Sorbonne. Certainly Fanon was addressing himself to the intelligentsia of the Third World,
and it is equally true that he made no concessions to the
"European" point of view. But there are several Eu-
ropes: did he not have in mind those Europeans who,
as he put it, "from time to time feel immeasurably
sickened"? One cannot deduce intention from results,
but it is undeniable that since his death Fanon has received more attention in the West than in the Third
World. In black Africa he has been subjected to silence
and neglect.

He died young. Simone de Beauvoir recalls him toward the end: "The conversation lasted until two in the
morning; I finally broke it off as politely as possible
by explaining that Sartre needed sleep. Fanon was outraged. . . . Like the Cubans, the Algerian revolution-
aries never slept more than four hours a night. . . . 'I'd

[19] Fanon, *The Wretched of the Earth*, pp. 252, 251, 254–55.

give twenty thousand francs a day to be able to talk to Sartre from morning to night for two weeks,' he told Lanzmann, laughing. . . . Everything he talked about seemed to live again before our eyes."[20]

His leukemia was acute, and he suffered a relapse. He went to Washington for treatment. He was left alone for ten days in a hotel room. His wife and six-year-old son joined him. The hospital changed all his blood and *The Wretched of the Earth* was published in Paris. His wife read him the first reviews to appear; they were enthusiastic. He loathed and distrusted America, which he regarded as a racist society. On his last morning, as he woke up, he said to his wife, "Last night they put me in the washing machine. . . ." He had caught double pneumonia.

He died in December 1961. The Algerians brought his body home by plane, and he was buried in Algerian soil, in a cemetery of the National Liberation Army. He was thirty-six.

[20] S. de Beauvoir, *Force of Circumstances* (New York, 1964), p. 592.

Fanon since Fanon

vii

The African peasant remains impervious to
Fanon, whose name is unknown to him. The
African elites turn their backs: they do not wish
to hear what he had to say. In America, meanwhile, the black militants discover Fanon. . . .

The majority of the African states today are
ruled by a single party or by the army. Roger
Barnard writes, "Yet throughout his [Fanon's]
work the single-party state remains an unquestioned assumption. . . ."[1] Irving Howe agrees:
"Fanon wants the masses to participate, yet
throughout his book the single-party state remains an unquestioned assumption."[2] And this,
in Howe's opinion, "means that the masses of

[1] R. Barnard, "Frantz Fanon," *New Society*, January
4, 1968, p. 12.
[2] I. Howe, *Steady Work* (New York, 1966), p. 77.

the people act out a charade of involvement but are denied the reality of decision." (Whereas, presumably, in Howe's native America, they act out a charade of decision but are denied the reality of involvement.) What does Fanon actually say? In Africa, he writes, "the single-party is the modern form of the dictatorship of the bourgeoisie, unmasked, unpainted, unscrupulous and cynical." And he adds, "All the opposition parties, which moreover are usually progressive and would therefore tend to work for the greater influence of the masses in public matters, and who desire that the proud, money-making bourgeoisie should be brought to heel, have been by dint of baton charges and prisons condemned first to silence and then to a clandestine existence."[3]

Fanon's ideal is a single, authentically revolutionary, peasant-oriented party. He was not an advocate of the single-party state as it was then developing in Africa, or of the cult of the leader. Kwame Nkrumah, known as "Osagyefo," "the Torch," and "the Messiah" variously, called Fanon his "friend." But Fanon clearly had the Osagyefo himself in mind when he described the typical African party leader as "the general president of that company of profiteers, impatient for their returns, which constitutes the national bourgeoisie. . . . His honesty, which is his soul's true bent, crumbles away little by little."[4]

Sartre's *Critique of Dialectical Reason* poses a dilemma. According to its socio-historical categories, a social class is a "collective" and a collective cannot rule; only a smaller, unified "group" can rule—for

[3] Fanon, *The Wretched of the Earth* (New York, 1965), pp. 132 and 147.
[4] *Ibid.*, pp. 146–47.

example, the Jacobins, the Bolsheviks, and the Fidel-
istas in Cuba. But groups are defeated by their own
victory: the period of revolutionary idealism gives
way to the inertia and egocentricity of power. After his
visit to Cuba in 1960, Sartre reflected, "What protects
the Cuban revolution today—what will protect it for a
long time, perhaps—is that it is controlled by the rebellion." Apparently this is what Fanon hoped for in
Africa. But such cases are rare.

Senghor equates all opposition with treason and sub-
version. "On this issue all indulgence would be a be-
trayal of the Nation." Sékou Touré: "The Party constitutes the thought of the people of Guinea at its high-
est level and in its most complete form." Nkrumah:
"The Party is the State, and the State is the Party."
John Tettegah, secretary-general of the Ghanaian
Trades Union Congress during the presidential election
of 1960, "We shall analyze the votes ward by ward,
and we shall know the places where the people have
refused to go and vote and they can be sure we will take
the necessary action against those traitors of our
cause. . . ." A few months later, with Ghana obviously in
mind, Fanon commented, "In those conditions . . . 99.99
per cent of the votes are cast for the governmental
candidate. . . . The Party leaders behave like common
serjeant-majors. . . ."

In the Congo, Dahomey, the Central African Republic, Upper Volta, Nigeria, Ghana, Sierra Leone, and
Mali, military coups. . . .

In the Arab states, it is sometimes difficult to distinguish between military and civilian government.
But everything is done in the name of the people.

Fanon foresaw this. He wrote that as the dictatorship of the single party hardens and as mass opposi-

tion intensifies, the army, led by an officer corps with a
supercilious caste spirit, would become the arbiter.
Latin American history, as he said, was repeating itself.

In fact, what is remarkable in Fanon is his insistence
on the need to separate the party from the government
and the administration. The party must not present any
careerist opportunities. It must be a means of discover-
ing and formulating the needs of the people; it must
be decentralized, drawing its inspiration from the regions and localities. He distrusted the bloated capital
cities. It was in the local branch meetings that the
peasantry would achieve a liturgical participation in
the handling of affairs; it was here that the pure,
austere fire of the nation would burn. This means that
Fanon, while not an anarchist libertarian calling for
the immediate destruction of all political and administrative institutions, did nevertheless share with liber-
tarians a basic distrust of what power does to men. He
talked in terms of collective responsibility at the base
and collegiate responsibility at the summit. Of course
this is easier said than done. How to reconcile planning
with democracy?

In one respect, Fanon was the Milovan Djilas of the
Third World. In *The Wretched of the Earth* he observed
and documented what Djilas observed and documented
in *The New Class*—the accession to power of a new
ruling class whose power was political rather than
economic. In Africa this class was largely congruent
with and developed out of the colonized national bourgeoisie. The new class legislates "socialism" in order
to control and plunder the national economy. "Scan-
dals are numerous, ministers grow rich, their wives
doll themselves up, the members of parliament feather
their nests, and there is not a soul down to the simple
policeman or the customs officer who does not join in

the great procession of corruption."[5] In the early 1960s, sixty per cent of the national budget in Dahomey was devoted to the salaries of government personnel. In parts of former French West Africa, parliamentarians who work only three months a year receive an annual salary equivalent to what a peasant of the region might earn in seventy-three years of toil. The fact that African leaders themselves sometimes draw attention to the phenomenon does little to halt it. In April 1962 Nyerere warned that privileged Europeans and Asians might soon be replaced by "a permanently privileged class of educated Africans." A year earlier Nkrumah told the nation on the radio, "I am aware that the evil of patronage finds a good deal of place in our society." Subsequently Ghanaian politicians were asked to surrender property in excess of twenty thousand pounds— a sum of money that a local peasant might accumulate in four hundred years if he saved every penny he earned.

Fanon in Africa—a voice in the wilderness.

But not in the United States. Dan Watts, editor of *Liberation* magazine, is reported to have told a journalist after the Newark and Chicago riots of 1967, "Fanon. . . . You'd better get this book. Every brother on a rooftop can quote Fanon." LeRoi Jones invokes Fanon, Stokely Carmichael calls him "one of my patron saints." Carmichael's emphasis is on the Fanonian break with Western values, the creation of a new Man, and the solidarity of black Americans with the people of the Third World. But here it is important to distinguish between the subjective and objective situations of American Negroes. Malcolm X called Third World solidarity and unity between black America and the

[5] *Ibid.*, p. 138.

Third World "a skin game." This was not what Fanon meant, but it could become that, and there is bound to be a developing sympathy among all those who have experienced the sting of white racial arrogance. But, turning to the objective sociological predicament, we find that Carmichael misrepresents Fanon when he declares that "the white American working class enjoys the fruits of the labors of the Third World workers. The proletariat has become the Third World, and the bourgeoisie is white society."[6] Fanon did not imply that. If white workers in America enjoy the fruits, then so do black ones, because they work within the same neocolonial economic system, if at a lower level. He described even the African proletariat as "the bourgeoisie" of the peasantry, and the African workers enjoy a lower level of life than do their black American counterparts. To quote Fanon: "The Negroes of Chicago only resemble the Nigerians or the Tanganyikans in so far as they were all defined in relation to the whites."[7] The later Fanon regarded racial oppression as a necessary but not sufficient definition of colonized status.

In one passage he hinted at the coming of armed violence by American Negroes, and there is no reason to imagine that he would have opposed it. On the contrary, he believed in social and racial violence on the part of the oppressed. As it happened, he suggested in 1960 that it might not be necessary—once again, the black American's predicament, in his view, differed from the African's. "The test cases of civil liberty whereby both whites and blacks in America try to drive back racial discrimination have very little in common in their principles and objectives with the heroic fight

[6] D. Cooper, ed., *The Dialectics of Liberation*, p. 165.
[7] Fanon, *The Wretched of the Earth*, p. 175.

of the Angolan people against the detestable Portuguese colonialism."[8] In other words, he did not foresee the rise of separatism and Black Power militancy in the United States. The black American writers whom he had heard and met at the Paris Congress of 1956 had impressed him as having attitudes, problems, and aspirations widely divergent from those of the colonial blacks. In *Black Skin, White Masks*, he had referred in apocalyptic images to the American racial battlefield, but he perceived a monument growing out of that bloody soil which promised to be majestic. "And, at the top of this monument, I can already see a white man and a black man *hand in hand*."[9] Had he lived longer, would he entirely have renounced that vision? Eldridge Cleaver's *Soul on Ice* strongly echoes the early Fanon's struggle for self-identification and self-assertion in a white culture. Cleaver's acknowledgment that "there is in America today a generation of white youth that is truly worthy of a black man's respect" perhaps offers a reprieve to Fanon's vision of the two races hand in hand.

Of course a book is both written and read, and even if it is not read very accurately its message, to a point, is what the reader makes of it. Thus when Carmichael and Charles V. Hamilton call themselves "African Americans" and refer to their "African cultural heritage," it may be irrelevant to object that Fanon regarded Negroism as a transitional cult which was already obsolescent. There is no sign or trace of any "African cultural heritage" in Fanon's own writings. But the objective role that such a skin-myth plays varies according to the situation and according to the general ideological structure of which it forms an element. The

[8] *Ibid.*, p. 174.
[9] Fanon, *Black Skin, White Masks* (New York, 1967), p. 222.

black American socialists such as Carmichael use it to develop the creative tradition of W. E. B. DuBois, whereas a politically disoriented black radical like Malcolm X could, and did, walk into a mirage.

Malcolm X was no doubt a brilliant and dedicated militant, and his release from what Cleaver appropriately calls "the racist strait-jacket demonology of Elijah Muhammad" was a breakthrough. Nevertheless, his account of his journey to Mecca, the Middle East, and Africa in 1964 would surely have appalled Fanon. Malcolm X discovered countries and cultures where white men and black co-existed in mutual dignity, and where black men were masters of their own nations. But the single-minded emphasis on skin and race led the spokesman of the Harlem Negroes to express deep gratitude for his reception by His Eminence Prince Feisal, deep gratitude for his lavishly entertained reception by the Honorable Kofi Baako of Ghana, and an even greater pleasure at being received in the presidential castle by Osagyefo Kwame Nkrumah—all men who represented a ruling caste that Fanon detested. It would seem, from his written account, that never, as he moved from airport to palace and palace to airport, did Malcolm X turn his head or his mind to the peasants hawking yams by the roadside. Malcolm X was traveling the dream corridors of the Emperor Marcus Garvey.

Fanon was a socialist; an enemy of capitalism, colonialism, and neocolonialism; a revolutionary; an antiracist who believed in the efficacy and humanist value of violent counterassertion; an opponent of authoritarian and elitist government, whatever its nominal label; and a champion of the poorest men on earth, the peasants of the Third World. Although his experiences, the agonies and humiliations of his own life, undoubtedly "belong" to the black people, his social philosophy is available to black and white people alike. He denounced Europe's record and Europe's applied values in the period of capitalist imperialism, but he did so in terms of the concepts of the European revolutionary tradition. There are no total hiatuses in ideological development; each new movement has roots in the old. Fanon added to that tradition and enriched it.

SHORT BIBLIOGRAPHY

NOTE: Translations are my own except where a published translation is indicated.

Fanon published two books and one collection of essays and articles in his lifetime. The books are:

Peau noir, masques blancs. Preface by Francis Jeanson. Paris: Editions du Seuil, 1952. Translated by Charles Lam Markmann as *Black Skin, White Masks.* New York: Grove Press, 1967.

Les damnés de la terre. Preface by J.-P. Sartre. Paris: F. Maspero, 1961. Translated by Constance Farrington as *The Wretched of the Earth.* New York: Grove Press, 1965.

The collected essays and articles were published as *L'an V de la révolution algérienne.* Paris: F. Maspero, 1959. Translated by Haakon Chevalier, with an introduction by Adolfo Gilly, as *Studies in a Dying Colonialism.* New York: Monthly Review Press, 1965.

A further volume of essays and articles, collected and published posthumously, is *Pour la révolution africaine*, Paris: F. Maspero, 1964. Translated by Haakon Chevalier as *For the African Revolution.* New York: Monthly Review Press, 1967.

For biographical and critical perspectives on Fanon, see:

Barnard, R. "Frantz Fanon," *New Society*, January 4, 1968.

Beauvoir, S. de. *La Force des Choses*. Paris: Gallimard, 1963. Translated by Richard Howard as *Force of Circumstances*. New York: Putnam, 1964.

Domenach, J.-M. *"Les damnés de la terre." Esprit*, April 1962.

Geismar, P., and Worsley, P. "Frantz Fanon: Evolution of a Revolutionary." *Monthly Review*, May 1969.

Gendzier, I. L. "Frantz Fanon: In Search of Justice." *Middle East Journal*, 1966.

Gottheil, F. M. "Fanon and the Economics of Colonialism." *Review of Economics and Business*, Autumn 1967.

Grohs, G. K. "Frantz Fanon and the African Revolution," *The Journal of Modern African Studies*, Vol. 6, No. 4, 1968.

"Hommage à Frantz Fanon." *Présence Africaine*, 40, 1962.

Nghe, N. "Frantz Fanon et les problèmes de l'indépendance." *La Pensée*, February 1963.

Pablo, M. "Les damnés de la terre." *Quatrième Internationale*, 15, 1962.

Rohdie, S. "Liberation and Violence in Algeria." *Studies on the Left*, May–June 1966.

Stambouli, F. "Frantz Fanon face aux problèmes de la décolonisation et de la construction nationale." *Revue de l'Institut de Sociologie*, No. 2/3, 1967.

Staniland, M. "Frantz Fanon and the African Political Class." *African Affairs*, January 1969.

Zolberg, A. "Frantz Fanon: A Gospel for the Damned." *Encounter*, November 1966.

Zolberg, A. and R. "The Americanization of Frantz Fanon." *The Public Interest*, No. 9, 1967.

INDEX